Praise for *Married to the Job*

"In this brilliant and deeply wise book, Philipson illuminates the new 'problem with no name.' Philipson is like an emotional union organizer, standing up for the rights of the 'work-divorced' and for long-hour employees with depleted nonwork lives generally. This book confirms and extends the findings of my own research and poses deep questions about a missing humanity in the lives we are invited to live. This is must reading!"

— ARLIE RUSSELL HOCHSCHILD, AUTHOR OF *THE TIME BIND: WHEN WORK BECOMES HOME AND HOME BECOMES WORK*

"Deeply disturbing and utterly convincing. Ilene Philipson shows us how and why America's long-workweek culture is wreaking emotional havoc—particularly in women's lives. Not surprisingly, workplaces (and bosses) cannot replace family and community in creating meaning and purpose in life."

— SYLVIA HEWLETT, ECONOMIST AND AUTHOR OF *CREATING A LIFE: PROFESSIONAL WOMEN AND THE QUEST FOR CHILDREN*

"*Married to the Job* is a sobering look at what happens to Americans when, as ties to family and community weaken, they overinvest in the workplace. Philipson holds that the problem lies not so much in the psyches of individuals as in a society where economic aggrandizement has come to dominate every sphere of life. She shows that we need not only individuals who can build a life outside work but a society that makes the economy the servant, not the master, of a fulfilling form of life. This is a book that cuts to the bone of the way we live now."

— ROBERT BELLAH, PROFESSOR OF SOCIOLOGY EMERITUS, UC BERKELEY, AND AUTHOR OF *HABITS OF THE HEART*

"If you think women work only because they 'have to,' Ilene Philipson has news for you: Growing numbers of women work long hours because the job has become their central source of community and human interaction. Enlivened with case studies and enriched with wide-ranging scholarship, *Married to the Job* is a groundbreaking study of workaholism—and of the loneliness that ultimately nourishes it."

—BARBARA EHRENREICH, AUTHOR OF *NICKEL AND DIMED*

"Philipson's wise and poignant book offers us a cautionary tale about the emotional dangers of being married to our jobs in today's one-night-stand economy."

—JOANNE B. CIULLA, PH.D., AUTHOR OF *THE WORKING LIFE: THE PROMISE AND BETRAYAL OF MODERN WORK*

"Well-researched . . . thoughtful."

—DIANE SCHARPER, *USA TODAY*

"Provocative . . . well-timed."

—ANDREA SACHS, *TIME*

"Many are likely to recognize themselves or someone they know in the patients described by Ilene Philipson."

—*THE TOPEKA CAPITAL JOURNAL*

"Calls into question those once-celebrated corporate cultures that inspire workers to blur the lines between life and work."

—*THE WASHINGTON POST*

ALSO BY ILENE PHILIPSON

Ethel Rosenberg: Beyond the Myths
On the Shoulders of Women: The Feminization of Psychotherapy
Women, Class, and the Feminist Imagination
(edited with Karen Hansen)

Married to the Job

Why We Live to Work and What We Can Do About It

ILENE PHILIPSON, Ph.D.

FREE PRESS

NEW YORK   LONDON   TORONTO   SYDNEY   SINGAPORE

*f*P

FREE PRESS

A Division of Simon & Schuster, Inc.
1230 Avenue of the Americas
New York, NY 10020

First Free Press trade paperback edition 2003

FREE PRESS and colophon are trademarks
of Simon & Schuster, Inc.

For information regarding special discounts for bulk purchases,
please contact Simon & Schuster Special Sales:
1-800-456-6798 or business@simonandschuster.com

Designed by Paul Dippolito

Manufactured in the United States of America

2   4   6   8   10   9   7   5   3   1

The Library of Congress has cataloged the Fress Press hardcover
edition as follows:

Philipson, Ilene J.
    Married to the job : why we live to work and what we can
do about it / Ilene J. Philipson.
        p.   cm.
    Includes bibliographical references and index.
    1. Workaholics. 2. Work—Psychological aspects.
3. Quality of work life. 4. Work and family. 5. Women—
employment—Psychological aspects. 6. Psychology,
Industrial.   I. Title.
HF5548.8 .P46 2002
158.7—dc21   2002068376

ISBN 0-7432-1578-8
ISBN 0-7432-1579-6 (Pbk)

Contents

Author's Note

Throughout this book, certain identifying information pertaining to my patients, such as names, occupations, ages, physical characteristics, and life histories, has been changed. Also, the names of the corporations for which my patients work are fictitious. Although I have occasionally grafted parts of one patient's experience onto another's, each clinical vignette represents the core story of an individual patient with details altered to prevent identification.

Neither the life of an individual, nor the history of a society, can be understood without understanding both.

—C. WRIGHT MILLS

To understand the dynamics of the social process we must understand the dynamics of the psychological processes operating within the individual, just as to understand the individual we must see him in the context of the culture which molds him.

—ERICH FROMM

Introduction

This book is about work and the ways in which it is colonizing our emotional lives. As we spend more time and energy at work, our jobs invade our dreams and fantasy lives, and define our identities. Paid work is increasingly where we get our emotional needs met and is surpassing neighborhood, community, and even family life, as the source of feeling alive and connected to others.

As a clinical psychologist whose psychotherapy practice is devoted to issues of overinvestment in the workplace, I have met with almost 200 patients who have turned to work for feelings of self-worth, guidance, passionate involvement in something larger than themselves, and/or simply having a place in the world, a way to identify who they are and how they fit in. Unfortunately, this overinvestment often has disastrous consequences. When all of one's life revolves around work, an insult or betrayal by a supervisor or coworker can be emotionally searing. If one feels ostracized from a workplace that has been the center of one's life, then friendships, community, personal identity, and even the very meaning of life, may suddenly rupture.

However, the increasing colonization of our emotional lives by the workplace is not merely an individual psychological issue. As I will argue, Americans' growing investment in work is a broad social current, one that is insufficiently recognized or understood. Divorce, the loosening of intimate ties, social frag-

I

mentation, and the decline of neighborhood, community, and civic participation propel us to seek meaning and sociability at work. Identification with one's corporation, feeling more alive in the workplace than at home, reliance on coworkers as one's primary source of friendship, tying one's self-esteem to a supervisor's approval, and total immersion in company culture as a substitute for embeddedness in community, increasingly characterize life in the United States today.

We are a nation in love with work. As stay-at-home mothers are viewed by many as, at best, anachronistic and, at worst, deficient; as welfare recipients are forced to join the paid labor force; as so many of us work longer hours and take fewer vacations, we express our heartfelt belief that work is fulfillment, mental health, moral virtue, and even the definition of citizenship. Our embrace of work is so fervent that, in the past few decades, we have redefined the very meaning of success. Formerly, personal success was evinced by the ability to *not* work, to be part of a leisure class, to be idle. Today, we measure our success by how *much* we work. We venerate the person who is so valuable and in love with her work that she arrives early and stays late at her job. The sixteen-hour day? That's heroic, impressive. As philosopher Joanne Ciulla has pointed out, previously, "people demonstrated their status through conspicuous leisure; today, people do it by conspicuous work."

Work has become something we do not merely for money, but for self-expression and self-actualization. This ideology has extended far beyond the professionals and artists with whom it long resided, and has spread throughout all classes in society. Simultaneously, feminism in almost all of its variations has prompted millions of women to view paid work as liberation and the means to equality with men. So thoroughly have we re-defined the nature of women's work in the past thirty years that, almost any time a woman makes a decision to not work in the labor force in order to engage in caretaking activity, she is viewed with suspicion and often condescension.

A recent *New York Times* survey of Americans' values revealed that "having a fulfilling job" was rated more highly than "being married," "being religious," "being a good neighbor," "being involved in the community," "having a lot of friends," or "having enough time for yourself."

This is not surprising, given that Americans are giving more and more time to their jobs. According to the United Nations International Labor Organization (ILO), by the year 2000, Americans on average were working 1,978 hours annually, up thirty-six hours from 1990. Based on the latest available information compiled by the ILO, the average Australian, Canadian, Japanese, or Mexican worker put in about 100 hours (about 2.5 weeks) less than the average American. Until the 1980s, Americans worked about the same number of hours as Europeans. Now we work on average "260 hours (about six-and-one-half weeks) more a year than British workers and 499 hours (about twelve-and-one-half weeks) more a year than German workers." Between 1977 and 1997, the average full-time workweek lengthened from forty-three to forty-seven hours.

A study of American workers found that 48 percent of women and 61 percent of men would still wish to continue working even if they had enough money to live as "comfortably as you would like." In another survey, which asked workers whether they preferred a shorter work week, a longer one, or their present schedule, "sixty-five percent preferred their schedule to remain the way it is. Of the remainder, three-quarters wanted *longer* hours. Less than 10 percent said they wanted a cut in hours." A 2001 study of full- and part-time workers found that 67 percent of those chosen at random say they feel *very committed* to their employers, up from 56 percent sampled in 1998.

In a comparative international survey of employees' attitudes toward work, Americans, British, and Germans were asked which of the following statements best described their feelings about their jobs: 1) "I work only as hard as I have to"; 2) "I work hard but not so much that it interferes with the rest of my life"; or 3) "I make a point of doing the best work I can *even if it interferes with the rest of my life*" (italics added). Sixty percent of Americans endorsed the third statement, whereas 55 percent of the British, and 37 percent of the Germans agreed. When working mothers are offered choices between benefit packages that allow them to stay at work more (e.g., on-site child care) or work less (e.g., part-time work or job sharing), women throughout the class hierarchy choose the former.

Since 1973, "free time has fallen nearly 40 percent." The majority of Americans do not take all the paid vacation time due them. According to a survey by Expedia.com, almost half of all full-time workers feel that they are too busy to take vacations. And, because of this, "we give back to our employers more than $19.3 billion a year in unused vacation time." However, it is not only the actual time at work that has increased. Commute time and the use of *electronic leashes*—cell phones, pagers, laptops, and e-mail—have increased the amount of time per day that we devote to work. As a study by AT&T discovered, "half of travelers either call in to work or check their e-mail while on holiday." The eight-hour day, punctuated by both weekends clearly partitioned off from work and vacations devoted to leisure, has become an American relic.

This relinquishment of leisure, this obsessive love of work, is new. In the earlier part of the twentieth century, people campaigned for the eight-hour day in order to have more leisure time, family time, personal time. Benjamin Hunnicutt, an historian of work, points out that progress "meant opening up life beyond the pecuniary—to family, community, the life of the mind." Having won the eight-hour day in the mid-1930s, a tremendous achievement for all working people in the United States, most Americans now seem to be turning back the clock to a time when employers controlled larger amounts of our waking hours. Without factoring in commute time or electronic-leash time, 46 percent of working Americans currently exceed the eight-hour day. And yet, there is no social movement, no protest, no public outcry. In fact, for many Americans having to confine work to the eight-hour day would be viewed as an unfair constraint, an impingement on their favorite activity.

Why is this the case? Why are we giving more of ourselves, of our time, to work—and with so little complaint?

The answer to this question is complex, because it resides within both our psyches and our social structures and institutions. In the pages that follow, I attempt to interpret our national obsession with work through the experiences of my patients. Their individual stories provide us with an entrée into understanding the ways social processes dwell within our psyches, and, in turn, how we continuously shape and reconstitute the social world in which we exist. If we as a people are increasingly living to work, we need to know what drives us on both an individual and psychological level, as well as on a social and cultural plane. While I do not discount economic insecurity, and the compulsion to consume in order to have things and status as reasons that compel us to work, what follows is an examination of our emotional needs, our yearnings and unconscious desires—a terrain rarely considered when thinking about work in American today.

CHAPTER ONE

Married to the Job

"I CAN'T BELIEVE THEY DON'T CARE!" This was Brenda's third session with me, and the same plaintive cry had echoed through my office in our two prior meetings. "I can't believe they'd do this. I feel like there's nothing to live for."

Thirty-five-year-old Brenda sat hunched over in the chair opposite mine. Tears streamed down her face; her eyes were red, swollen; her long blond hair appeared matted in places. She stared out, looking somewhere above my right shoulder. It seemed my function was to bear witness to the tragedy that had unexpectedly seized her and transformed her life into a barren, thinglike existence. Brenda had been betrayed at work and, because of this, she simply saw no point in continuing to live.

When she walked into my psychotherapy office one week earlier, she had sobbed wordlessly for the first twenty minutes of our session. Slowly, in tear-drenched staccato, Brenda was able to tell me the outlines of her fall from grace, her workplace agony. In our second meeting, I gathered the basic sweep of her life history, the history that seemed to have found its culmination in her exile from the law firm in which she worked. I did not know it then, but this narrative of a coherent and productive life suddenly disrupted by a betrayal at work was one with which I would gain increasing and intimate familiarity. It was

Brenda's story that began to transform my understanding of the role work plays today in our lives, in the very core of who we are as human beings.

Brenda grew up in an intact, working-class family. Although her father was an alcoholic, and she was one of six children who received little attention from either of her working parents, Brenda graduated high school with honors and immediately began work as a receptionist at age eighteen. During her seventeen years in the labor force, Brenda steadily worked her way up the clerical hierarchy, becoming a legal secretary for a small, very prestigious law firm, earning almost $50,000 per year.

Brenda's life beyond work was stable and relatively free of conflict. She had been divorced for seven years, owned a one-bedroom condominium, and had been in a relationship with a divorced man, Barry, for three years. Brenda described Barry as "very nice . . . , cares about his kids . . . , likes the simple things in life." Brenda's own family lived in another state, so she rarely saw them, given her commitments to work and to Barry.

Brenda idealized the attorneys for whom she worked: Their upper-middle-class lifestyle—season tickets to the opera, weekend homes in the mountains, active involvement in the alumni associations of their alma maters—brought Brenda into intimate contact with a world to which she had no former exposure. "These guys didn't care about money. They *assumed* it. They cared about better things. They had ideals." One of their "ideals" was continual self-improvement, and, to this end, they paid for Brenda to attend weekend seminars in the Napa Valley once a year to learn how to become "self-actualizing" and more effective at work. In response to this kind of interest in her, her relatively high salary, and her involvement in a workplace that, to her, seemed "about as posh as you can get," Brenda happily worked fifty to sixty hours per week, ran personal errands for her employers, and always spoke of the law firm in the first-person plural: "We're going to court on Monday"; "We had the office painted."

After working at the law firm for four years, Brenda had to miss the annual company Christmas party because her mother had had a stroke two days before. It was Brenda's responsibility to plan and execute the party to which clients were invited, a task she readily assumed, even though it was not part of her job description. After quickly making arrangements with two other secretaries to handle her responsibilities for the party, Brenda flew home to be with her ailing mother. When she returned to work one week later it was as if "my whole world had collapsed." Her employers were very upset with her. There had been a number of foulups at the party, and they blamed them on her ill-timed departure. The attorneys appeared cold and unresponsive in their interactions with her. They began asking another secretary to do their errands, and Brenda's favorite attorney gave this same secretary spare tickets to a sold-out play in San Francisco that Brenda longed to see.

Brenda developed insomnia; she stayed awake at night ruminating about what was happening at the office. She went over and over the way in which she had handled arrangements for the party, and blamed herself for the problems that had occurred, for leaving to see her mother. She developed migraine headaches for the first time in her life, frequently felt nauseated, and began to lose weight. Increasingly, she cried at work. She would sit on the toilet in the women's restroom and sob. There were days when her headaches were so incapacitating that she called in sick. After two months of enduring this agony, Brenda went to her doctor, who signed her off on short-term disability and referred her for psychotherapy.

In the course of the week in which we began meeting, Brenda cut herself off from her boyfriend because she felt profoundly misunderstood by him. Neither he nor anyone else could grasp why she was so upset. Barry repeatedly suggested she get another job, telling her "It's just a job; get over it." But, for Brenda, it wasn't "just a job"—it was her life.

In our first few sessions together, I was unable to fully understand and enter into Brenda's experience—her despair, her agonizing language of terror and loss, her overpowering feelings, which filled my office. In truth I understood Barry's position far better than Brenda's: It *was* just a job. Why did this betrayal signal the end of her life? How could anyone be so terribly upset over what happened at work? And, of course, as my lack of understanding continued, Brenda's suffering only worsened and her symptoms, and their dramatic expression, escalated in her increasingly desperate attempt to enlist my empathy and help.

One day, the patient I met with directly before Brenda was a woman in her thirties going through a particularly painful and acrimonious divorce. In this case, it had been clear to me that the sudden departure of this woman's husband, who had left her for a mutual friend, precipitated a devastating personal loss, leaving her with profound feelings of shame and a terrifying sense of isolation and confusion about who she was without her husband. My immediate acceptance and understanding of her reactions allowed this woman some sense of soothing, and a reduction of her shame and panic.

In the following hour, while bearing witness once again to Brenda's agony, I was struck by the remarkable similarities in her and my previous patient's experience. After a while, I simply stated that it was as if Brenda had been married to her law firm, and that, suddenly and without warning, her husband told her that he didn't love her anymore and was leaving her for another woman. This rather simplistic intervention had the effect of stopping Brenda's tears and capturing her imagination. For the remainder of the hour Brenda and I built and embellished this metaphor. Twice during the session she made clear to me that her "real divorce" from her husband seven years prior "wasn't anything like this one. I could never care about a man like I cared about [her law firm]." I acknowledged this and stated that I didn't see why a divorce from a job wouldn't be just as horrible, and perhaps worse, than a divorce from a spouse. Although, at that point, I didn't quite believe what I was saying, at the end of our session Brenda arose from her chair for the first time without tears streaming down her face. As she opened my office door to leave, she turned around and said calmly, and with obvious relief, "I guess I was sort of married to my job."

LIVING TO WORK

It is a common belief that Americans work longer hours because we are a consumerist, avaricious people who see work as a means to garnering possessions. Our materialistic culture inflames our desires for more, bigger, designer-labeled, luxurious, brand-named stuff. We'll do whatever it takes to be able to consume what we want.

But, strangely, no one I have seen in psychotherapy has ever discussed consumption in connection to what propels them to invest in their jobs. Rather, they are more likely to speak of emotional longings—for recognition, self-esteem, a sense of belonging, or purpose—that they seek to fulfill at their workplaces.

As so much of our family and community life has become less vibrant and emotionally rich, corporations became not just places to work but places to live during the 1990s. In order to attract, retain, and keep employees working longer hours, many companies began offering amenities, activities, a sense of being valued and belonging that hooked people in emotionally. Free food, weekly parties, and on-site child care, to cite just a few examples, bind people both physically and emotionally to their workplaces. Company logos and slogans that surround employees and pervade our culture often are all individuals can identify with, claim as their own. Corporations can feed our unmet longings with countless exhortations that "We Are A Team!"; "We're Number One!"; "We Are Fam-i-ly!"

In the face of home life that is often little more than a refueling station centered on running errands and watching TV, or "community" life that frequently consists only of shopping in the local, chain-dominated mall, the workplace offers embeddedness in social relationships, involvement in company gossip and intrigue, the opportunity for both individual and collective achievement, and recognition for that achievement. In some sectors of the economy, corporations are campuses with gymnasiums, massage therapy, gourmet food, and concierge services. As arranging mergers, taking companies public, satisfying the needs of venture capitalists, meeting shareholders' expectations, and competing globally speed up our economy, working today can resemble contributing to a passionate crusade. It not only taps into the needs unsatisfied by family and community, it provides us with involvement in something larger than the self, involvement previously satisfied by religion, trade unions, volunteer organizations, and social movements.

Acknowledging the emotional grip that work has on so many of us is not something I have come to readily. As a clinical psychologist, I was trained to closely investigate the inner workings of family life in order to understand personality formation, and see how people replay childhood dramas in their adult lives. Work, if anything, was secondary. Insofar as it had any psychological meaning, it was an empty or blank arena in which people could play out unresolved conflicts, conflicts entirely rooted in families of origin. Thus, I was woefully unprepared when Brenda first came into my office. It had been only two months earlier that I had taken a position in a large group practice that serviced the mental health needs of most of the HMOs insuring patients in the Berkeley–Oakland area.

Previously, in community mental-health settings, I had seen a predominance of seriously mentally ill and drug-dependent clients. Conversely, in private practice, I met with people who wanted to improve the overall quality of their lives, overcome lifelong, self-destructive patterns, or unearth the causes of their pain founded in unhappy or abusive childhoods. But it was in this new group practice setting in which working people accessed their HMOs to see a therapist that I encountered Brenda. My initial impression was that her plight was unique. As my caseload increased, however, I began hearing more and more about work not as background, but as the focus of distress, hope, longing, and simply interest in people's lives. And it is these patients' stories—revealed, examined, puzzled over in psychotherapy, that have slowly wrested my attention away from the family as the emotional hub of life and redirected it toward the workplace—the workplace as the repository of people's emotional needs. Brenda's psychological dependence on her job became the template for, rather than the exception to, my new patients' narratives.

Within two months of Brenda discovering that she was "married to her job," I received six more referrals of female patients whose stories strangely paralleled Brenda's. The paths these demographically diverse women took to my office were relatively uniform: They were referred by their primary care physicians after repeated visits to their doctors' offices complaining of diarrhea, headaches, muscle tension, insomnia, heart palpitations, nausea, high blood pressure, numbness in their extremities, uncontrollable crying, and/or irritable bowel syndrome. Having ruled out any clear physical etiology for these problems and/or met with a total lack of success in treating them, the physicians urged these women to seek psychotherapy and referred them to my group practice.

Upon arriving at my office, most seemed to be suffering from a major depression or anxiety disorder. Some spoke in voices loud with alarm, announcing that they couldn't believe what was happening to them, that their worlds had turned upside down. For others, their voices were locked inside them, and they choked off bits of words, informing me that their lives had ended; they had no future. They sobbed and shook, or appeared numb and motionless. Their stories contained few relatives, social friends, spouses, children, or clergy. Home life simply did not appear in their renditions of the tragedies that had befallen them, even though many were married and/or had children. There was a single subject that dominated their thoughts and their words: Work. Betrayal at work.

Initially, I regarded these women with wonder. After having largely consistent and unremarkable work histories, each described experiencing some kind of insult, anger, or lack of empathy from her supervisor or coworkers (e.g., she was yelled at, questioned about her ability to perform a task, asked to work overtime when returning to work from an illness, not invited to a coworker's lunchtime birthday party). With often great emotion, each of these women explained how her employer "turned against me," "knifed me in the back," or "didn't even care." They often expressed amazement at being treated coldly or harshly by a supervisor or coworker whom they had considered a friend, fictive family member, or idealized parental figure: "She used to treat me like a sister." "He always talked about us being one big family." "I looked up to these people!" "I knew I was his favorite secretary." "I thought the world of my boss." Despite my successful intervention with Brenda, I continued to think that the seeming devastation each of these women felt was out of proportion to the injury she had suffered.

Apparently, my initial response mirrored that of these women's families and friends. Although some reported that they had told no one about their employment tragedies, those who had were typically greeted with something similar to what Barry had told Brenda: "Just get over it and get back to work." Husbands, mothers, girlfriends, even doctors, didn't understand why these women continued to be symptomatic and virtually unable to focus on anything other than the betrayal at work. This lack of understanding served to underscore a tremendous feeling of isolation and hopelessness.

This sense of emotional disconnection was magnified by these women's inability and/or refusal to return to work. Most were far too physically and emotionally disabled to do their jobs. Their diarrhea or headaches or sobbing prevented them from leaving their homes. Their depression or anxiety impeded their concentration, short-term memory, and capacity to engage in social relations. So, they left work on short-term disability, they stayed home, and their sense of isolation and disconnection from the world of work, that is, the world of the living, escalated.

My bewilderment at their plight only increased as I learned more about them. Most had weathered numerous stressors in their lives: single motherhood, divorce, death, alcoholic parents, childhood sexual abuse, rape. However, nothing seemed to compare with the current pain, that is, the pain of being shouted at or ignored by the people at work.

Truly at a loss to help them, and because each of these women seemed to feel so utterly alone in her suffering, I decided that they might be able to help each other. I started a group that I advertised "for women who are unable to work due to problems with their supervisors or coworkers." Since its inception in February 1993, over 150 women have participated in this group-psychotherapy program. It is through facilitating these groups that I have seen how work can, and has, become home, salvation, human connection, and identity to many in our society.*

Within a few years of starting my group-therapy program, I began writing for both professional and popular publications on the psychology of work. As a result, I started receiving phone calls from men and women who wondered if they were "married to their jobs" (a phrase I had used frequently in my writing), that is, overinvested in work, even though no betrayal had yet occurred. I began meeting with people from all profes-

---

*I discuss this group therapy program at length in Chapter Six.

sional categories—chief financial officers to data entry clerks—
who came to therapy describing a similar phenomenon: Work
had eclipsed every other arena of life and penetrated to the core
of their emotional lives. It had become what they thought
about when they woke up in the morning and dreamed about
at night. Children and spouses were often regarded as secondary in importance to work's overwhelming pull. Frequently,
the forty-hour work week was considered part time. Sex was a
distant memory. Often, there were no friends or activities beyond work, and even time itself was measured by a project,
company meeting, or party. Extracompany events such as
Thanksgiving or New Year's might be spent at the workplace,
and children's birthdays celebrated with special trips to
mommy's or daddy's office.

In the spring of 2001, I began receiving an increasing number of new referrals of men and women who had been laid off.
They had committed themselves without restraint to workplaces that had been riding the crest of the economic boom.
And, suddenly, their worlds crashed down around them as the
economy soured and then, later in the year, the World Trade
Center was destroyed. These patients' sense of betrayal often
extended beyond the confines of their particular workplace to
their very faith in an economic order that seemed to have offered continuous growth and endless possibility.

What all of these patients described going on with them at
work was not workaholism. They were not addicted to the
content of their work but, rather, deeply emotionally attached
to their *workplace*. That attachment and dependence seemed to
consist of many ingredients: the work setting, the social relationships within which the job was embedded, the sense of
identity that emanated from being employed by a particular

corporation or institution. Being married to one's job is no more an addiction than marriage to a spouse. It is a total personal commitment, a fundamental constituent of one's identity. It is based on both emotional and economic dependence, and comes first in one's commitments, in sickness and in health.

When Brenda described what she missed about her job, it was not her actual work as a legal secretary. Instead, she missed the attorneys, whom she had idealized. They had affirmed and appreciated who she was, and introduced her to ideals and a sense of purpose larger than the self. She missed her fellow secretaries, who had become friends she talked with every day. When she would tell them about problems she might be having with Barry, they would take her side, often telling her "you don't deserve that," or "he's lucky to have you." Comments such as these allowed Brenda to feel more confident and substantial in her relationship with her boyfriend.

Perhaps most important, Brenda identified with the law firm as an institution or total environment. She experienced an enormous sense of pride when she told others the name of the firm for which she worked, given its prestigious reputation in the community. She would cut out newspaper clippings that contained references to the law firm, and luxuriated in the posh physical environment of her workplace. Brenda's attachment to the firm was not merely an emotional and economic one; it was also remarkably sensual. She described the smell (a melange of expensive cologne, leather, and gourmet coffee), the feel (of leather chairs, thick carpets), and the sounds (KDFC, the local classical music station, playing in the background). As in any marriage, Brenda's wedlock spoke to a variety of psychological needs and longings that were satisfied nowhere else in her life. Without her job, Brenda indeed believed that her life was over.

"I Owe My Employer Everything"

In the years since I first met with Brenda, I have seen patients from a wide variety of backgrounds enter my office. The similarity of their presentations has persuaded me that Brenda's plight resonates broadly within our society. Ingrid, Lionel, and Sarah all were married to their jobs.

Ingrid represents another end of the continuum. She has never been betrayed by work and feels she is at the top of her game. Ingrid, however, is just as married to her job as is Brenda. The only difference is that she doesn't yet know it.

Ingrid called me to set up an appointment after reading an article about my work in a business magazine. She said on my voice mail that she felt her life was "out of balance," and she wanted to see me because the article had led her to believe that I might understand her "devotion to work."

When Ingrid entered my office I was struck by this very attractive woman's faultless appearance. She wore an expensive tailored suit; her hair was a perfect brown bob; nothing was creased, askew, or less than understated elegance. As Ingrid spoke she revealed herself to be an extremely intelligent, articulate, thirty-nine-year-old woman, who, it seemed, had annexed her very being to the workplace.

Ingrid had grown up in an upper-middle-class community, the daughter of professionals who emphasized hard work, achievement, and living a productive life. Throughout her teens and early twenties she felt comfortable both being pro-

ductive and having fun. She received excellent grades, but was
also a high-school cheerleader and a sorority sister at the Ivy
League college she attended. She had boyfriends, drove a sports
car, and did drugs recreationally while in college.

She feels that her life began to change when she entered an
MBA program at one of the nation's leading business schools.
The competition was intense, and the requirements of studying
and working diminished the time and energy she had for her
social life. Upon receiving her master's degree, she was hired by
one of the largest, well-established Silicon Valley corporations.
Ingrid worked there for four years, steadily moving up the corporate ladder, working long hours and thinking of little else
besides her responsibilities, her interactions, her standing at
work. "Here I was at twenty-eight making over $100,000 a
year and they think I'm great! I can do no wrong. I'm hot!"

Ingrid was lured away from her job by a start-up company
that I will call E-Stream. She took a significant pay cut in order
to work with E-Stream, but explains: "I never had time to
spend the money I was making anyhow [laughs] . . . This was a
real chance to make a difference . . . I liked their vision . . . It
made me feel in the morning that I could change the world."

In order to "change the world," Ingrid worked 110 hours a
week. She describes sleeping on the conference-room floor for
four hours in her clothes each night, then freshening up in the
bathroom. The venture capitalists who were funding E-Stream
would drive by the company on the weekends or at night and,
if they didn't see enough cars in the parking lot, they would
complain to Ingrid and others, questioning their commitment,
and wondering how the venture could ever go public without
its employees' requisite dedication. Because she was one of the
few women at E-Stream, Ingrid feels that she drove herself

harder than many of her male colleagues. She lost weight, never talked to friends or family, and one day found her tropical fish dead because she had neglected to feed them.

E-Stream did have a public offering and is now one of the most successful corporations in Silicon Valley. Ingrid is one of its vice presidents and proudly tells me that she never works more than eighty hours a week. She came to therapy at thirty-nine because she feels her devotion to work has "interfered with my outside life."

To fully understand the enormity of this statement one must know that Ingrid has no social contact outside work, and no one she can point to as a friend. She has not had sex in eleven years. She typically spends Christmas or New Year's at work, where, she states, "there's always something going on." At times, Ingrid feels that her attachment to work is excessive, that there's something wrong with her, that she's "missing something, like a boyfriend or having children," and it is these concerns that brought her to see me. However, she also describes a remarkable sense of fulfillment, mastery, and connection at work:

"It's like nothing else, going public and being at a company like this . . . We set the pace; we're making history . . . I love the people I work with . . . So many of us have been through it all and we still respect each other and work well together . . . I know you think it's crazy I work so much, but it's not like I'm sitting at my computer all day. A lot of it's talking to really smart people about what we're going to do, where we're going to go. I don't think some *relationship* [with contempt] or a bunch of rug rats are exactly going to make me feel that good, at the top of my game, you know?"

During the same week I first met with Ingrid, I received a phone call from Lionel. In our brief conversation Lionel told me he had never been to see a "shrink," but that his doctor thought it might be a good idea for him to talk with someone as soon as possible. Lionel stated that the rug was pulled out from under him at work, and he was at loose ends because of that.

When Lionel first walked into my office, his head nearly hit the top of the doorway. He is a very tall, lean, outgoing man with a wife of twenty years, a stepson, and a home in the sub- urbs. He has worked for one of the largest corporations in the Bay Area, which I will call VPA, for twenty-seven years. His is a true American success story, rising from warehouse worker to data base manager. Lionel feels tremendous loyalty to his employer. His emotional dependence on his job transcends any feeling he has had for another human being. "They made me what I am. Without their faith in me I'd probably still be work- ing minimum wage. I love my wife, but I owe [my employer] everything."

At his workplace, every employee, including the CEO, oc- cupies a certain level on a scale of one to one hundred. Within each level, an employee is ranked on a one to five scale, accord- ing to job performance. Lionel became obsessed with levels and rankings. He was a "fifty-nine," his supervisor was a "sixty- three," and Lionel hadn't seen any advancement in three years. Therefore he continually ruminated about how to advance his career "to leave the fifties."

When a job interfacing with a new computer system be- came available within the company, Lionel applied. Although he admits he wasn't truly qualified for the job, he pressured the department that was hiring to give him the position. "It was my ticket. I'd automatically be a sixty-three."

Once in his new job, however, Lionel was overwhelmed. He didn't understand the new system and was too afraid to ask questions, fearing that those who had hired him would immediately see him as what he thought himself to be, a fraud. He struggled, developed chronic neck and shoulder pain, and found himself increasingly irritable with his family. For the first time in his life he felt capable of road rage as he sat in his car, commuting two hours each way to the corporation that, he stated, "made me what I am."

Three months into his new job, Lionel was sitting in a team meeting with his new supervisor, a man fifteen years his junior, with an M.B.A. from a prestigious school. The supervisor stared at Lionel for what seemed to be an eternity and then, according to Lionel, asked him for a report, his voice dripping with sarcasm. Lionel began to hyperventilate, had to leave the room, and rushed to the company nursing station in a full-blown panic attack.

Lionel's doctor placed him on short-term disability due to his newly diagnosed and uncontrolled high blood pressure and his panic disorder. Lionel feels he cannot return to his workplace because he is humiliated. He believes there is no other job for him, despite the fact that he possesses excellent computer skills and lives in an area where such skills are in high demand. The rage at his new supervisor, whom Lionel feels shamed by, is palpable. Lionel states that he can identify with men who go to the workplace and kill supervisors and coworkers out of feelings of betrayal: "I *get it.* I never could understand that kind of thing before this happened to me . . . What, you're just supposed to sit there and take it?" Lionel fantasizes about beating up his supervisor and plays over and over in his mind what happened at the meeting at which he felt so humiliated.

Lionel grew up in a stable family, but one in which strong emotions were eschewed and praise rarely given. He had been an average student, whose only real success in high school had been playing on the varsity basketball team. When he began work in VPA's warehouse, however, he found a supervisor who was very impressed with his work habits, his willingness to work overtime and help out in different departments, and his physical strength. Lionel quickly was promoted, and had a series of supervisors who encouraged and praised him. By his own admission, he increasingly lived for that praise. VPA's rankings and levels symbolized the esteem and approval Lionel cherished.

Lionel describes his home life as "okay." His stepson is in his early twenties and still lives at home. Lionel states that he never truly became a father to him, although he has lived with him for twenty years. "I worked so much and for the last twelve years have had this bitch of a commute . . . And, when I was around, I guess I kinda left my heart at work . . . I would be throwing a ball with him, but my mind would be somewhere else. You know, the current project, how things were going."

Lionel's investment in people or activities outside work has been slight. He has depended on VPA for the satisfaction of most of his emotional needs. Although his wife has shown herself to be caring and loving, and Lionel has tremendous appreciation and respect for how supportive she has been during his current period of disability, their marriage simply does not offer the emotional nourishment Lionel craves. "If she says something I do is good, that's just her opinion, plus she's my wife, she has to say that (laughs). But coming from them (his employer), you know that really says something." What it seems to say to Lionel is that an authoritative, prestigious, and powerful institution says he is good, worthy, smart, successful, and, I think, a man. Because of his dedication to his employer, Lionel has never looked for any other source to help bolster his sense of self. Without his job he feels lifeless, deflated, with only his abiding anger connecting him to his lifeline, VPA.

Sarah's workplace was not far from Lionel's. A thirty-three-year-old single mother, Sarah had worked for six years at what I will call "PeoplePoint." She adored her job as office manager. She worked six days a week, often twelve hours a day, because, she claimed, she was "needed" and "felt so appreciated." Her appreciation certainly did not consist of a high salary nor a generous vacation. Sarah earned about $36,000 a year and never took a day off. The appreciation she experienced was the accolades management would shower on her, the roses she was sent by the various teams with which she interfaced, and the leftovers her direct supervisor would bring her from his lunches with clients. "I honestly thought that I was so special because *I* got the Chinese food in those little white boxes," she stated.

Sarah would bring her two small sons to work with her at night and on the weekends. She would dress them in People-Point clothes, which were available in the company logo store. She covered her house with PeoplePoint items and had her sons saying they wanted to work at PeoplePoint when they grew up. She routinely used her own money to buy muffins and bagels for the staff, remembered coworkers' and supervisors' birthdays, and planned various company activities, such as pumpkin carving contests and holiday parties.

After some serious mistakes in acquiring two smaller companies, PeoplePoint began laying off employees for the first time in its history. Sarah was asked to take on departed coworkers' tasks, and she acquiesced without thinking. However, as her responsibilities grew, Sarah found herself unable to

keep up with the workload. She couldn't sleep and felt perpet-
ually anxious and exhausted. After a couple of months spent in
this state of chronic stress, Sarah gently approached her supervisor, and asked if she might be relieved of some of her new duties. Her supervisor responded with a single admonition: "If
you can't stand the heat, get out of the kitchen." Sarah states
that she "nearly passed out when he said that. I couldn't believe
my ears. After all I had done for them, and this is what I get. I
mean, they didn't care that I was falling apart, that my kids
didn't really have a mother." Two weeks later, Sarah received a
layoff notice and, shortly thereafter, walked into my office. She
says that separating herself from PeoplePoint is far more difficult than her divorce: "My husband was just a man and I know
there'll be other ones out there. But I know there'll never be another PeoplePoint."

Sarah describes a lifelong desire to be needed and to help
others. She grew up in a large family and found her place, her
identity, through being supportive and useful. She felt close to
her sisters, always surrounded herself with friends and never
had difficulty attracting male attention. After three years of
college, Sarah dropped out of school to marry her boyfriend.
Soon thereafter, she moved with him to a community about an
hour-and-a-half from where she had lived her whole life, so
that he could enter a residency program at a teaching hospital.
She then became pregnant and stayed home to take care of her
first, and then second, son. Sarah looks back at this time in her
life as a lonely one, separated from family and friends. She had
worked part time through high school and college and found
taking care of her home and children unchallenging and insufficiently engaging.

When her sons were two and four, Sarah took the job at

PeoplePoint and quickly discovered the challenge and emotional engagement for which she had been longing. As an expanding company that was continually reinventing itself, PeoplePoint made great use of Sarah's seemingly endless willingness to work at any task to which she was assigned. Sarah reflexively responded to the total company culture that emphasized the "PeoplePoint family" and "PeoplePoint values." She was appreciated for how homey she made the workplace: Coworkers and supervisors would flock to her office because of her warm personality, her eagerness to listen to anyone's problems, and the candy bowl on her desk, stocked with treats. She actively transformed the workplace into a more homelike environment, not only by bringing in cut flowers and bagels, but by binding people together through having them sign greeting cards when coworkers were ill or had babies, planning lunches for employees' birthdays, and soliciting input for how the next party or company social event should be structured.

Once Sarah started working long hours at PeoplePoint, she and her husband simply never saw one another. His long hours as a physician took him away from home much of the time. Their children were in full-time child care and, often, would sleep in sleeping bags next to Sarah in her PeoplePoint cubicle as she toiled in the evenings to finish a project. After about two years of this thoroughly alienated family life, Sarah's husband announced he was in love with another woman and requested a divorce.

Sarah states that her life as a single mother does not feel appreciably different from that as a married woman, given the high degree of emotional disconnection she experienced from her husband. Her real love was and is PeoplePoint, a company that provided her with a sense of family, community, self-esteem, and the sense of purpose for which she longed. The conundrum that Sarah's story, and so many others', reflects is that, the more we invest in work, the less time and emotional resources we have to invest in family and community. In turn, this decline in investment depletes our small family units still further, causing us to rely more heavily on work in an attempt to satisfy our unmet longings and needs.

The Continuum of Emotional Investment in Work

So, what can people like Brenda, Ingrid, Lionel, and Sarah tell us about Americans' obsession with work? How can such extreme stories illuminate the more common, mundane experience of our daily trips to and from the office? Can viewing the workplace from the unusual vantage point of the "analytic couch" tell us anything about where we are headed as a society in our relationship to work?

I have come to believe that my patients' situations—often so extreme and so difficult for others to understand—are embedded in Americans' increasing reliance on the workplace for the satisfaction of our emotional needs. I would suggest that, if we regard these patients as forming a distinct psychological syndrome or disorder rather than representing a pole on a continuum of emotional investment in work, we miss what their experience can teach us.

From a purely clinical point of view, it is possible to see these patients having incomplete or incohesive selves, dependent upon external sources for esteem and a sense of personal well-being. Identification with the job itself, the company, or a supervisor may provide substance, a way of anchoring the self in a more firmly established person or entity. "It was the first time I ever had a business card. There I was in black and white: Marion Richards, Account Manager," one woman told me. Another said: "When I was around Larry [her boss], I felt safe." And, of course, Lionel's comments regarding VPA making him "who I am" all suggest a reliance on work to prop up one's self, one's identity, one's sense of security in the world.

However, to view this psychological reliance in only a clinical fashion can obscure what these individuals' experiences may reveal about the larger meaning of work in our lives. If we assume that Brenda, Ingrid, Lionel, and Sarah represent a point, perhaps an extreme point, on a continuum that measures our dependence on work for the satisfaction of many of our most basic emotional needs, then they may provide insight into Americans' more general infatuation with work. Just as the plight of Freud's hysterical patients shed light on the conflicts of middle-class Victorian women in general, the experiences of the patients I see may illuminate more widespread problems in our society's relationship to work.

In Freud's treatment of hysteria, his consulting room became a locus for those experiencing the brunt of Victorian mores—economically privileged women who were expected to suppress and repress sexuality, ambition, vitality, aliveness. Their multiple, often bizarre, symptoms acted as physical, nonverbal protestations against their confinement, against their oppression as women. None could directly articulate the source of their pain, in part because their suffering was located in the very foundations of their culture, its values, its understanding of what it was to be a member of society. It is arduous indeed to stand outside of prevailing norms, to gain perspective on the dominant culture and see how the water in which one swims may be toxic.

In similar fashion, the patients I see may bear the brunt of our current obsession with work. Each has given him or herself completely, unselfconsciously, and without self-protection, to work. They idealize their companies or supervisors without restraint. They exhibit almost a Calvinist approach to working hard and being personally productive. They do not view themselves as being out of step with our society's values but rather *epitomizing* those values through their dedication to their jobs. After a period of disability, and upon being hired by a new corporation (for which he was working sixty to seventy hours a week as Director of Information Technologies), a patient told me:

"It's like a life raft, you know, because I felt like a total loser before, like I really didn't belong on this planet. But it's so cool. I'm always thinking, 'What's the best step for the department to take next,' how maybe I can get a leg up, be more creative, work a little harder. It's good to feel you're giving it all."

From where I sit—near the geographic boundary of Silicon Valley—giving it all to our jobs increasingly appears to be a widely accepted American value, a sign of success, of virtue, certainly of necessity, in our fast-paced, globalizing new economy. There are few voices asking if working fifty, sixty, seventy hours a week is pathological. Taking work on a vacation? Talking on a cell phone to coworkers while sitting in a restaurant? Making the company Christmas party the most anticipated social event of the year? These actions are not considered extreme, or even unusual. We have come to accept being married to our jobs as a necessary fact of life in the twenty-first century. It is in this light that I would argue that my patients' stories, their anguish and emotional upheaval, is one end of a continuum on which most Americans can locate their own experience of work.

However, in giving it all to our jobs, we are running a great risk. As Americans are working longer hours and investing emotionally in our jobs, we are simultaneously depleting our lives beyond work. As corporate teams, departments, supervisors, and coworkers monopolize people's emotional resources, personal relationships outside the workplace are drained of vitality, and participation in neighborhood, community, or civic life wanes. This process feeds on itself. As life outside the job becomes less compelling, more anemic, there is simply less to come home to and less to go out to. A family life centered on errand running and watching television, or a community life based on trips to the mall and the cineplex simply can't compare to the centripetal pull of the workplace.

When work fails—through a betrayal, rupture, or layoff—employees who have given it all often find there is nothing to fall back on. In the case of Sarah or Ingrid, there are no relationships outside the workplace to offer solace, or even perspective, on their overinvestment in their jobs. Even when there are supportive, understanding family members or friends to turn to, these relationships often do not seem to provide the necessary emotional nourishment. In Brenda's case, her boyfriend Barry's inability to understand her total dependence on her job made her feel that he was inadequate, uncaring, unempathic. Lionel's wife, conversely, was resolutely supportive, patient, and accepting, but Lionel had never invested in his marriage in the way he had invested in VPA. Thus, anything she said held less meaning than that which Lionel felt was being communicated to him by his employer. He had placed his value as a person in the hands of the company for which he worked, and no mere mortal outside VPA—even his wife—could dispel the power he had given to his employer to define him and his worth as a human being.

This handing over to corporations the power to define us and our worthiness is dangerous from the individual's, the corporation's, and society's, perspective.

As my patients' stories demonstrate, if work is used as the primary means to achieve an identity, a sense of self-worth and belonging, when it fails, a psychic death or emotional collapse can occur. An abyss, a bleak landscape without purpose looms. After leaving PeoplePoint, Sarah explained, "suddenly everything seemed gray. I mean everything. The flowers, clothes, even the sky." Brenda, like virtually all my patients, couldn't imagine doing anything that could give her pleasure or a sense of truly being alive outside of work. "Everybody works, so where would I go, what would I do, who would I see?"

The only means my patients have of understanding a failure at work is in individual, shame-drenched terms. They feel excluded from their workplace home, from their source of vitality, goodness, meaning. Even if they are angry, on some deep level they blame themselves and feel humiliated by their sense of being workplace exiles or outcasts.

This sense of individual responsibility is a fundamental part of the American tradition. However, it is intensified by the demise of countervailing institutions that might provide an understanding of what happens at work. At other points in our history, institutions such as the family or trade unions were powerful enough to root our identities, and offer a vision of a meaningful life outside the job. If an employee experienced a workplace failure, being a wife or a father or a member of the working class could provide identity, a sense of belonging, but also a means of viewing the workplace from the vantage point of an institution that was filled with import and meaning. The family or the union symbolically could say "You belong here; you have a role. From here, we can look at VPA or PeoplePoint and tell them with authority that they do not define the world."

Without those institutions speaking to us in that fashion, we are left with only ourselves to blame. There is no language provided anywhere to label or give shape to our personal sense of failure. So, falling ill, becoming depressed or impotently enraged, and developing symptoms that are at once physical and psychological often becomes our only means of expression. As the keen observer of the modern workplace Richard Sennett has observed:

> Failure is the great modern taboo. Popular literature is full of recipes for how to succeed but largely silent about how to cope with failure. Coming to terms with failure, giving it a shape and a place in one's life history, may haunt us internally but seldom is discussed with others . . . As with anything we are afraid to speak about forthrightly, both internal obsession and shame only thereby become greater, left untreated is the raw inner sentence "I am not good enough."

Ironically, an employee's being married to his or her job can have deleterious effects for corporations, too. Creating total company cultures intended to attract, retain, and keep employees working incessantly can backfire. Emotional dependence on one's job can create working relationships that are brittle and subject to sudden rupture when an employee feels let down. A corporate or managerial decision that is based exclu-

sively on business criteria can be interpreted as personal and ·
emotionally laden if an employee believes the company is her
family. When work is one's lifeline to feelings of esteem, self-
worth, and belonging, any kind of real or imagined disruption
in that lifeline can result in an employee feeling betrayed, hurt,
or angry.

As my patients' stories demonstrate, the most productive
people can be lost to the job when they feel their implicit marriage contract with their employer has been altered or severed.
They can be less productive, call in sick, or go on disability. They
can turn from being invaluable employees to recipients of private, state, or workers' compensation disability payments and
high utilizers of the health- and mental-health-care systems.
And, in the worst-case scenario, they can react to feeling betrayed by acting out violently against their employer. In the majority of cases of disgruntled workers committing acts of violence
against supervisors or coworkers, the employee seems to have felt
betrayed by someone, most often his supervisor, at work.

Lastly, it is society, our social fabric, that is compromised
by our overidentification with and emotional dependence
upon our jobs. As we give more of ourselves to work, we lose
sight of our need for connection with others that used to develop in neighborhoods, extended families, congregations,
PTAs, local bars, fraternal organizations, and picnics in the
park. We lose sight of our need for recognition for who we
are, rather than for what we do; for attention and acknowledgment unmediated by corporations, that is, by instrumental
interests that view people only as employees whose worth is
ultimately measured by their contribution to the bottom line.

As our identities verge on becoming corporate constructions, we lose our capacity not only to be actively engaged family members, but citizens. The larger social good in a democratic society can only be served by citizens who are simultaneously embedded in, and autonomous from, the institutions around them. Unlimited emotional investment in the workplace hampers that autonomy and reduces our ability to participate in civil society. When we give it all to our jobs, there simply is little left over. Our emotional reserves to care for each other—within families and within society in general—are depleted and impoverished. Living to work impedes our capacity to develop a vision of life and of how it should be lived. When we tether ourselves to the workplace and cannot see beyond the next deadline, the next promotion, the next company event, we lose sight of ourselves and our place in the world.

In asserting this, however, I want to be clear that emotional overinvestment in work cannot be understood exclusively as an individual's responsibility on the one hand, nor as a function of corporate intervention and control on the other. We cannot understand our growing reliance upon work without understanding the social forces that compel so many of us to rely psychologically on the workplace. Turning to our jobs for the satisfaction of emotional needs is a societal problem, one that has as much to do with what has happened to our families and communities as with what goes on at the workplace. Thus, we now turn to the question of how we make sense of Americans' desire to spend more time at their jobs, take fewer vacations, remain electronically leashed to their workplaces, and wake up in the morning and go to sleep at night thinking about their jobs. We turn to life outside the workplace, a life that for many has *less to come home to* and *less to go out to*.

CHAPTER TWO

Less to Come Home to/
Less to Go Out to

Work as a concept can be understood only if there's something
other than work against which to measure it.
— JONATHAN KEATS

IN THE PAST THREE TO FOUR DECADES, life outside of work
for many of us has become increasingly anemic and drained of
vitality. Both family and community have lost part of their hold
on the emotional lives of many Americans, providing us with
fewer norms and values with which to understand the world
around us. Separateness, anonymity, fragmentation, and im-
permanence increasingly characterize our experience.

Until quite recently, social theorist Max Horkheimer's as-
sertion that "The present-day family is a source of strength to
resist the total dehumanization of the world," could be taken as
a truism. It was in our families and local communities that a
sense of permanence, security, and acceptance could be sustained. At their best, these institutions fostered reciprocity, loyalty, solidarity, and resilience. In practice, real families could be
the source of pain and abuse, but the ideal of what a family or
community *should be* exerted a pull that allowed us to observe
the total dehumanization of the world with some perspective.

This perspective is now diminished. As political scientist

Robert Putnam declares in his comprehensive work on community life in America, *Bowling Alone:*

> For the first two-thirds of the twentieth century a powerful tide bore Americans into ever deeper engagement in the life of their communities, but a few decades ago—silently, without warning—that tide reversed and we were overtaken by a treacherous rip current. Without at first noticing, we have been pulled apart from one another and from our communities over the last third of the century.

As author Brian Robertson has noted, the latter third of the century stands "as a cultural turning point of the most profound significance, when the old, uneasy balance between domestic and marketplace spheres began to break down." What Horkheimer observed as the bulwark against the intrusion of market forces increasingly *mirrors* those forces. Many Americans view the likelihood of maintaining sustained and intimate ties with others over time with the same insecurity with which they view the marketplace.

It was not so long ago that complete spontaneity, absolute autonomy, and being freed from obligation and constraint, appeared to be the hallmarks of personal liberation. However, freedom to move away from family ties assumed the endurance and durability of the family. We could define our newly liberated selves in contrast to an institution that seemed permanent and unyielding. As it turns out, family and community have proven to be far more fragile than many of us could ever have imagined. Personal freedom is harder to achieve in a landscape of dislocation and weak ties.

In the 1960s, posters, greeting cards, self-help books, and even coffee mugs carried the message of freedom from constraint and the glorification of the chance encounter. Fritz Perls' "Gestalt Prayer" summarized what would soon serve as a general view of intimate relations in America:

> *I do my thing, and you do your thing,*
> *I am not in this world to live up to your expectations,*
> *And you are not in this world to live up to mine,*
> *You are you and I am I.*
> *And if by chance, we find each other, it's beautiful,*
> *If not, it can't be helped.*

While many Americans today probably have only a foggy memory of this so-called prayer, its message has penetrated deeply, and, simultaneously, reflected accurately, our current stance toward romantic entanglements and meaningful human ties in general. What Perls, the father of the Human Potential Movement, promoted was a world filled with unconnected individuals who live outside "expectations," who do not encounter each other intentionally, through planning or with hope, but only "by chance." If we never experience such an encounter, thus if we remain alone, we are helpless to alter this fate. We glide on the surface of life without hope and without despair. There can be no critique or even evaluation of a social fabric so thin, so insubstantial. It simply "can't be helped."

In this gossamer landscape of chance encounters, the structured world of work with its expectations, regularity, and opportunity for camaraderie and belonging, looks pretty attractive to a lot of people. Given that the "Gestalt Prayer" did not create but only reflected and promoted a cultural turning point of the most profound significance, we must ask how we arrived at a place where relationships are so ephemeral, and where such precariousness goes unquestioned. As we look at the transformations of our family and community life over the past thirty years, we visit a terrain that has become increasingly denuded by Americans' investment in work and, in turn, offers less to people when they return home from the job. There is no simple issue of cause and effect here. When we examine the relationship between family and community and work, we see a reciprocal movement of people away from families and communities into the workforce that thereby diminishes life outside the job. As we will see in chapter 4, in a globalizing economy, corporations demand and encourage such movement, so much so that our long work hours and emotional commitment to our work deplete our families and communities still further.

LESS TO COME HOME TO

A little over twenty years ago, I could stand in front of a lecture hall teaching students of the sociology of the family that there were two universal principles that had forged the institution of the family over time. One was the principle of legitimacy: The family served to establish who was a legitimate member of society. Those born outside its marital contract were illegitimate and, hence, inherently unfit to participate in the social life of a community. Second was the principle of reciprocity: The family was the arena in which men and women reciprocally exchanged their labor to produce the necessary goods and services that allowed for survival. Women gathered; men hunted. Women spun wool; men tilled the fields. Women raised the children and went to PTA meetings; men worked full-time at large, bureaucratic corporations. Although there could be endless variation in family structure and function, these principles appeared transhistorical and transcultural.*

Within a remarkably short period of time, these principles have been negated. Over the past thirty years, the concept of illegitimacy has been rendered meaningless and anachronistic, and the assumption that women and men need to rely on each other for survival is clearly obsolete. Both the idea and the reality of family life have radically changed. Over the course of the last quarter of the twentieth century, instability, fragility, singleness, and isolation have grown as characteristics of family life in the United States.

Clearly, there is no single cause for the loosening of these bonds. Any historical account of what has fundamentally transformed family life would need to address the fall of the breadwinner ethic, women's increased labor-force participation, the rise of the contemporary feminist movement, the divorce revolution, and the widespread acceptance of being single and living alone.

From the mid-nineteenth century until quite recently, the American economy was based on the *family wage,* that is, male workers were paid enough to support a wife and family. Although for many in our society this remained more of an ideal than a reality, the family wage materially anchored certain values and norms that were generally shared throughout American society. A man's proper role was that of provider for his family. Women and children were his dependents. Gender formed the basis of a strict division of labor that dictated not

---

*These principles were denoted by anthropologists Bronislaw Malinowski and Claude Levi-Strauss, respectively.

only who had direct access to making money, but what it meant to be masculine, feminine, single, childless, productive, and an appropriate member of society. Sociologist Jessie Bernard writes:

> To be a man one had to be not only a provider but a *good* provider. Success in the good-provider role came in time to define masculinity itself. The good provider had to achieve, to win, to succeed, to dominate. He was a bread*winner* . . . Countless stories portrayed the humiliation families underwent to keep wives and especially mothers out of the labor force, a circumstance that would admit to the world the male head's failure in the good-provider role.

The breadwinner ethic served to trap both men and women in confining, restrictive gender roles. While men were consigned to a lifetime of labor, solely responsible for the survival of a wife and children, women were rendered economically and emotionally vulnerable. If unable or unwilling to attract and/or keep a man, they faced entry into a labor market that paid them less than men. As Barbara Ehrenreich points out, "The other side of the principle that a man should earn enough to support a family has been that a woman doesn't need enough to support even herself."

Simultaneously, we can now see that the breadwinner ethic also provided real stability for many in our society, and a generally shared ideal for how to live, how to connect, how to build families. Certainly, such an ethic excluded homosexuals and those who were systematically excluded from equal access to the labor market, such as African-American men. However, it served as a moral force that governed rules of courtship, obligation between the sexes, responsibility for children, and the care of dependents. It dictated the distribution of material and emotional resources within the family and within society in general. It was confining and burdensome, but it anchored the intimate ties for most Americans in a moral code of reciprocity, loyalty, and obligation over time.

The breadwinner ethic collapsed in the 1960s and 70s. Survey data reflect the enormity and abruptness of this change. In comparing attitudinal surveys conducted in 1957 and 1976, Jessie Bernard reports that, in 1957, 68 percent of working men had "a positive attitude toward marriage." Remarkably, this declined to only 39 percent by 1976. Similarly, the "proportion of working men who found marriage and children burdensome and restrictive more than doubled, from 25% to 56% and from 25% to 58%, respectively." During this same time the percentage of married men who saw marriage as "all burdens and restrictions" rose from 42 percent to 57 percent. And 45 percent of married men saw children as "all burdens and restrictions" in 1976, while in 1957, 28 percent had.

Bernard concludes that the breadwinner ethic officially died in 1980, "when the census declared that a male was not automatically to be assumed to be head of the household." Author Barbara Ehrenreich elaborates on this change:

> In the 1950s . . . there was a firm expectation that required men to grow up, marry and support their wives. To do anything else was less than grown-up, and the man who willfully deviated was judged to be somehow "less than a man." . . . But by the end of the 1970s and the beginning of the 1980s, adult manhood was no longer burdened with the automatic expectation of marriage and breadwinning. . . .

I . . . want to impress on you the profundity of the change represented by the collapse of the breadwinner ethic. In the space of a few decades, our culture has inverted the expectations that made the family wage system in any sense justifiable as a means of distributing wealth from those who are relatively advantaged as wage earners to many of those (women and children) who are not. Men still have the incentives to work and even to succeed at dreary and manifestly useless jobs, but not necessarily to work *for others.*

To work for others, to be a good provider, entails a willingness to care for one's dependents, particularly one's children, over time. It implies a readiness to put their needs ahead of one's own interests and desires. Therefore, one means of gauging that the breadwinner ethic, that is, working *for others,* has little salience in many families today is to look at what happens to fathers' financial support for their children after divorce. Once the marital tie is broken, we can see how tenuous the connection between fathers and their offspring can be, in that 40 percent of children who are eligible for child support receive no legal award. And, for children who are legally entitled to their father's support, a quarter receive nothing and less than one-third receive the full amount awarded to them.

This neglect of *working* for others is also mirrored by fathers' neglect of *caring* for others, as reflected in contact between fathers and children following divorce. A national survey of one thousand children from disrupted families reveals that almost half of the children living apart from their fathers had not seen them in the previous year; fewer than half had *ever* been in their father's home, and only one-sixth had seen their father once a week or more in the previous year. In a typical month, two-thirds of the children had no contact with their fathers at all. For children whose parents had been divorced ten years or more, only one in ten had weekly contact with their fathers and almost two-thirds had no contact with their fathers in the previous year. Sociologists Frank Furstenberg and Andrew Cherlin, who reported on this survey, conclude that these "Findings provide an especially bleak prognosis for long-term relations between fathers and their offspring. Over time, the vast majority of children [of divorce] will have little or no contact with their fathers."

With the demise of the breadwinner ethic, the participation of women in the labor force necessarily rose dramatically during the latter part of the twentieth century. When we look at the effects of this on the family, mothers' work outside the home is particularly relevant. In 1950, 12.6 percent of women with children under seventeen worked in the paid labor market. By 1998, 73 percent did, and 62 percent with children under one year of age worked outside the home. Rather suddenly, men weren't just married to women; they were married to fellow workers.

While the sociological literature makes clear that the vast majority of women who entered the labor force in the 1960s and 70s did so for economic reasons, feminism and new paradigms defining psychological health provided ideological justification and personal meaning for this movement.

The postwar economic boom of the 1950s and '60s ended abruptly in the mid-1970s. Due to oil price increases, a slowdown in productivity growth, heightened international competition, and sluggish demand, the median income for American families began to fall, and the majority of employees saw their average wage peak in 1973, then decline throughout the 1970s and '80s. In order to maintain their standard of living, American families responded to the economic downturn by sending more family members, that is, women, as well as teenagers, into the paid labor force. Thus, as men's and women's attitudes toward the breadwinner ethic were changing, economic realities and beliefs about sex roles were shifting as well. More wives were working outside the home, because their husbands could no longer provide the standard of living that had become expected in the postwar boom. Unlike earlier in the century, men were not denigrated for their failure to fully support their wives and children.

This movement of women into the labor force was not motivated by material factors alone. Beginning in the late 1960s, most forms of feminism began to define women's autonomy and, often, liberation in terms of equal labor-force participation. Increasingly, anything less than full-time work has served to call into question a woman's self-respect and commitment to herself. In just one generation what it is to be a woman—and what it is to be a man—has been redefined. To be economically dependent is to be weak, immature, parasitic. Interestingly, just at a time when the economy needed more workers, and families needed to send more members into the workforce to retain their standard of living, feminism offered women's labor-force participation as the *sine qua non* of equality and liberation. As the institution of the family was weakening, as a result of the decline of the breadwinner ethic and the dramatic increase in hours spent at work, feminists were characterizing the family as a locus of oppression and the workplace as the seat of liberation. Feminist social movement theorist Barbara Epstein has explained this by noting:

It is always the first task of a movement to attack oppressive institutions that are in decline. To the extent that they are anachronistic they can be shown to be illegitimate; it is possible to turn public sentiment against them with relative ease . . . It is the weakness of the institution that makes such an assault possible . . .

Thus, seeing the family in largely oppressive terms, while equating paid work with liberation, obscured the serious fault lines that were appearing in increasing numbers of American families. This perspective also cloaked the problems inherent in viewing the workplace as the site of personal freedom. Rather than critically questioning the idea of giving all of ourselves to our jobs, feminists embraced the workplace wholeheartedly. It was there that women could finally discover both equality with men and a kind of self-realization and fulfillment unavailable in the domestic sphere. In this way, feminism incorporated many of the tenets of therapeutic discourse in the United States as it has evolved since the 1960s.

During the latter part of the twentieth century, both popular psychology and more traditional forms of psychodynamic and cognitive therapy have emphasized continuous personal growth, self-fulfillment, autonomy, and freedom from guilt as hallmarks of psychological maturity and health. The human potential movement of the 1960s and '70s popularized an extreme version of these ideas that coincided with the burgeoning feminist movement's emphasis on women's independence, individualism, and self-expression. An excellent example of this psychological stance is the popular 1971 book by David Viscott, *Feel Free: How to Do Everything You Want Without Feeling Guilty*. In his introduction, Viscott virtually approaches his readers with contempt for remaining committed and loyal when they could be devoted to personal growth and fulfillment:

> The chances are . . . you'll stay in the same situation, in the same role, in spite of how much you hate it. You'll stay married to the same person, no matter how many reasons you can give for leaving. You'll put off all the things you really want to do . . . Why is it that you haven't grown out of it? Why is it that much of the time you aren't really doing what you want, aren't really happy where you are or whom you are with? What's holding *you* back?

While ostensibly offering an attack on guilt, the message that Viscott and his contemporaries conveyed simply replaced one kind of guilt with another. Rather than feeling guilty for leaving one's spouse, shirking one's responsibilities, or acting impulsively, the psychologically healthy person now had to feel guilty for staying put, for not doing everything he or she wants.

Given the rigidity of roles and the narrowness of attitudes that pervaded post–World War II American culture, this psychological framework spoke to people's real needs and dilemmas. It also, however, encouraged ephemeral relationships and the loosening of strong ties. As the equation of emotional maturity with self-expression and freedom from constraint has permeated our culture, divorce, fathers' abandonment of children, and even working long hours and leaving children for most of the day in child care can be justified by the need for personal growth and fulfilling one's potential. Obligation and responsibility have been recast as repression and an unwillingness to be autonomous and grow.

This shift is most clearly revealed in our acceptance of divorce as a normal part of adult development. Divorce rates doubled in ten years, between 1965 and 1975, and continued upward until they stabilized at around half of all marriages in the early 1980s. "As a consequence of this sharp and sustained rise," notes Barbara Dafoe Whitehead, "divorce moved from the margins to the mainstream of American life in the space of three decades." The author of *The Divorce Culture* goes on to note that this mainstreaming of divorce "suggested that relationships themselves—especially relationships that are binding or permanent—are risky investments. The most reliable form of investment thus becomes the investment in the self." What this suggests is that as men and women feel freer to leave unsatisfying marriages, that very freedom can then act as a constraint: to be truly vulnerable to another, to feel deeply connected and desire commitment over time puts one at risk, emotionally and, sometimes, economically. Therefore, we must constrain our desire for commitment and permanence, narrow our expectations, and see in every relationship that fails, the opportunity for more personal growth and greater investment in the self.

Given the risks involved in intimate relationships, remaining single has come to make a good deal of sense, and that is precisely what greater numbers of Americans are doing. We are spending less of our lives in marriages than ever before. The proportion of people who are currently married fell from 74 percent in 1974 to 56 percent in 1998. In 1957, 53 percent of Americans believed that unmarried people were "sick," "immoral," or "neurotic," and only 37 percent viewed them "neutrally." By 1976, 51 percent viewed them "neutrally;" 33 percent viewed them negatively, and 15 percent saw them in a more positive light than their married counterparts. In 1972, 45 percent of American households were composed of a married couple with children. By 2000, 23.5 percent were. Today there are more one-person households than ever before. In 1960, 13 percent of all households contained only one person. By 1998, 26 percent did. Thus, for the first time in American history, households composed of a single person are more common than those with a married couple with children.

As family bonds shrivel, and security through intimate relationships recedes from our experience, investing in the self through investing in one's work can often seem like our most viable option. Brenda made this choice. After her seven-year marriage ended in divorce when she was twenty-eight years old, she read self-help literature and engaged in "soul searching." She concluded from this experience that "I can't go down that road again. I have to think about what's best for *me,* how I can take care of myself." She decided to implement this decision by buying her own one-bedroom condominium, finding a job she truly liked, and vowing never "to let myself get caught up with somebody like I did with Steve [her ex-husband]." In many ways, Brenda's disillusionment with marriage and her aversion to going down the road of sustained and enduring relationships made her particularly vulnerable to the vagaries of her job. However, given our current social landscape, with its limited opportunities for anchoring the self and resisting the total dehumanization of the world, it is unclear what better choice Brenda might have made.

Home Alone

A little over two years ago, I first met with Luba, a proud, middle-aged woman, to talk about the betrayal she felt she had experienced at her workplace. Her seeming total absorption in work concealed another story, however. This more hidden story was about family, and how the current configuration of the intact, nuclear family can leave its members feeling isolated and deadened. When we feel there is little to come home to, work beckons.

Four years prior to entering my office, Luba was hired to work as a systems analyst at a large software company. Her workplace was not a nondescript office building in the middle of the city, but a multi-acre "campus" which seemed at once bucolic and exhilarating. Luba, who holds a doctorate in computer science, immediately found herself in a work group of highly educated men and women who were under constant pressure to complete a never-ending succession of projects. For months at a stretch, she would work twelve-hour days and spend weekends working from home on the computer her employer had provided. Luba states that she loved her work and became deeply involved in the lives of her coworkers, most of whom were from India, and who seemed to use Luba as a confidante. When not thinking about the content of her work, she worried about her coworkers whom she describes as "really wonderful people; although some of them seemed to me lonely and sad." Often late at night, or on the weekends, Luba e-mailed her coworkers, and discussions begun at work continued throughout the week so that work enveloped her life—a seamless web of real and virtual community.

Luba spent over three years in this fashion, describing them as the happiest she had ever experienced. Then came March 6, 1998. This is a date Luba repeats at least once in every psychotherapy session. It was on "that horrible date" that Luba was reassigned to another work group, without warning and without any opportunity to resist. She felt wrenched out of an environment of inclusion and camaraderie, only to be placed in a new group that was filled with acrimony, petty rivalries, and big egos.

Even though this transfer represented a new level of responsibility and increased pay, Luba began to resent the corporation she had loved. She hadn't been consulted about the transfer; she missed her prior coworkers terribly; no one cared about her plight. She ruminated, fretted, and slowly began to seethe. She became irritable and short with her new coworkers and started experiencing a plethora of physical symptoms: shortness of breath, headache, heartburn, numbness, and tingling in her hands. In response to these symptoms, Luba's doctor insisted she take some time off work and seek psychotherapy to deal with her festering anger. Since then, she has not returned to her job. She remains angry and hurt, feeling that her life has "no meaning or purpose . . . I feel like a shell of a person. There's nothing left."

One of the most salient facts about Luba, and about most of the patients I treat who feel betrayed by their jobs, is that she does not cleave to work because she is literally alone in the world. Rather, Luba is in a marriage of fifteen years and has a son who is twelve and a daughter who is eleven. She and her husband emigrated from an Eastern European country fourteen years ago in order to seek greater career opportunities. They have been enormously successful in pursuing their goal, and have a lifestyle that most Americans would envy.

At the same time, a certain sense of emptiness, of routinization and sameness, seems to pervade Luba's home life. Given that both Luba and her husband have always worked at demanding professional jobs, her children became accustomed, virtually from birth, to having highly structured lives that fit into the requirements of their parents' work schedules. Luba describes her children as very self-sufficient, and engaged in a wide variety of extracurricular activities that take them—like their mother and father—away from home for most of the day. Aside from the ritual of attending weekly soccer games, Luba's family members spend weekends engaged in separate activities. When they are home together, each typically is locked away in his or her own room, either online or watching television alone.

Luba states that she loves her family and that they are her highest priority. However, they remain virtually absent from the highly dramatic content of her psychotherapy sessions, and do not seem to provide her with the meaning and purpose for which she longs. At work Luba felt needed, praised, involved, intrigued, energized, and immersed in a total community of likeminded people. The constant pressure of project completion and the fascination with which she regarded the vagaries of her coworkers' lives seem to have allowed Luba to feel alive in a manner she had not previously experienced. Her nuclear family does not seem to supply the emotional exhilaration that work does.

Luba's family life seems to mirror that of an increasing number of Americans. As more of us work and work longer hours and as technology increasingly saturates our home lives, fragmentation and isolation can make home a pretty empty place. If most family members spend the majority of their waking hours away from their homes and come back feeling spent, only interested in watching TV or checking e-mail, it is difficult to invest in family life.

Today, fathers of children under eighteen work on average 50.9 hours per week, and mothers 41.4 hours per week. Married couples averaged fourteen more hours at work each week in 1998 than 1969, and one-fifth of all working parents work opposite shifts, so that they are rarely home at the same time.

Due to these kinds of work schedules, children spend more time in child care or alone at home than ever before. The White House Council of Economic Advisers found that American parents on average spend twenty-two hours less each week with their children than their counterparts did thirty years ago.* As Juliet Schor points out:

> [T]he most alarming development may be the effect of the work explosion on the care of children. According to economist Sylvia Hewlett, 'child neglect has become endemic to our society.' A major problem is that children are increasingly left alone, to fend for themselves while their parents are at work . . . Local studies have found figures of up to one-third of children caring for themselves. At least half a million preschoolers are thought to be left at home part of each day. One 911 operator reports large numbers of frightened callers: "It's not uncommon to hear from a child of six or seven who has been left in charge of even younger siblings."

A recent report from the U.S. Census Bureau indicates that 6.8 million children, five to fourteen years of age, are regularly left at home unsupervised while their parents are at work or away for other reasons. At the same time, the average Ameri-

---

*"But," according to Robert Reich, "this doesn't necessarily mean that each child is losing twenty-two hours of attention, because adult Americans are having fewer children to begin with." (Reich, op cit, p. 119)

can teenager now spends approximately three-and-a-half hours home alone each day and spends more time by him or herself than with family or friends.

Even when family members are home at the same time, they are more likely to be alone, apart from each other. "Virtually all forms of family togetherness became less common over the last quarter of the twentieth century. Between 1976 and 1997, according to Roper polls of families with children aged eight to seventeen, vacationing together fell from 53 percent to 38 percent, watching TV together from 54 to 41 percent, attending religious services together from 38 percent to 31 percent, and 'just sitting and talking' together from 53 to 43 percent."

In this climate, the family meal increasingly is anachronistic. Over the last twenty years, married couples who report that their families eat together have declined from 50 percent to 34 percent. By 1997, spending on takeout meals and restaurants exceeded spending on groceries. These facts lead Robert Putnam to conclude that since "the evening meal has been a communal experience in virtually all societies for a very long time, the fact that it has visibly diminished in the course of a single generation in our country is remarkable evidence of how rapidly our social connectedness has been changing."

Even the geography of family life has been altered. Generally, we live in larger houses with fewer people. The average single-family house increased to 2,190 square feet in 1998 from 1,500 feet in 1970. Simultaneously, the average number of children per household decreased from 2.44 to 1.85. Witold Rybcznski, author of *Home: A Short History of an Idea,* states that, with "physical separation comes isolation. And if the family isn't together, they can't talk." Commenting on the trend in new home construction to have children's bedrooms placed on the opposite end of the house from their parents', Rybcznski says: "Architecturally, these houses are very similar to wealthy Victorian homes. The difference is that in the Victorian era, servants, maids and governesses monitored kids. Now, the kids are often alone."

With increased isolation, family members turn to television and the Internet, thereby becoming more isolated from each other and from their communities.

The average American watches television four hours per day. Three-quarters of American homes have more than one set. The fraction of sixth graders with a television in their bedrooms rose from 6 percent in 1970 to 77 percent in 1999. Increasingly, Americans do not sit down to watch particular shows, but like to watch whatever's on, as evidenced by the fact that those of us who turn on the TV with no particular program in mind jumped from 29 percent in 1979 to 43 percent by the end of the 1980s.

A large number of the patients I see talk about television personalities as if they were family members. It is as though these personalities have replaced the kin and friends who might have dominated one's thoughts in previous times. It appears that many families now silently and passively watch TV sitcoms in which fictional families laugh, chat, emote, and struggle with each other. The actual family members' needs for affective connection is enacted for them while they sit disconnected, often in separate rooms.

Sharon, a forty-seven-year-old CFO, would often tell me about the travails of television characters she watched nightly after returning from her ten-hour work days. Her husband, a psychiatrist, read or wrote in his study, while Sharon took over the bedroom to spend the evening in front of the television. Another patient told me that after writing code all day for his job, he liked nothing better than to return home to watch old sitcoms such as *I Love Lucy* and *The Brady Bunch*. When I asked him where his wife and children were during these times, he replied "I don't know. I guess doing chores and stuff."

The ways in which TV's fictional families serve to replace actual families' affective ties was conveyed poignantly to me by Marion, a forty-one-year-old, single mother of two teenage daughters. Marion had spent her twenties on drugs and welfare. Her daughters were often cared for by relatives as she went through drug rehab, then by a college daycare center as Marion worked on her B.A. By age thirty-eight, she had become a corporate account manager, and ultimately ended up in one of my groups after feeling betrayed by her job. Marion often commented on how she regretted not spending more time with her children. Today, each of her daughters has her own room and spends virtually all of her time talking on the phone or in online chat rooms. Marion insists, however, that the three of them spend Friday nights together to eat takeout pizza and rent videos. Although they often disagree on what films to rent, they all have a favorite: *The Godfather.*

I really love those scenes with Marlon Brando and Sonny and all of them together. It's all shot in those brown, antiqued tones that make it seem so homey and warm. My daughters really like them too. We must have rented those a dozen times . . . *Godfather III* I don't like as much. It's sad the way Al Pacino has nothing in the end. He spends his whole life trying to hold the family together and look where it gets him. I'd say we've rented that a couple times. We mainly watch the first one, then the second one. It just makes us feel good. It makes us all feel good.

While the similarities between this African-American family and that of the Godfather seem few indeed, I think the breadth and depth of the Godfather's family relationships evoke for Marion a rich and intense home life for which she and so many others yearn. In listening to Marion over the course of two years, hearing about her upset with her workplace, as well as her feelings of alienation from her daughters, I believe those Friday nights watching *The Godfather* were among the very few events in Marion's life that brought her anything close to contentment and a real sense of connection with her children.

Use of the Internet is a new way of spending time at home alone. In one of the first surveys of the effects of Internet use conducted by Stanford University's Institute for the Quantitative Study of Society, it was demonstrated that "the Internet is causing many Americans to spend less time with friends and family, less time shopping in stores and more time working at home after hours." Norman Nie, political scientist and principal investigator of the study, concludes that "the more hours people use the Internet, the less time they spend with real human beings." The Internet is creating "a broad new wave of social isolation in the United States, raising the specter of an atomized world without human contact or emotion . . . If I go home at 6:30 in the evening and spend the whole night sending e-mail and wake up the next morning, I still haven't talked to my wife or kids or friends." Nie believes that with increased use of the Internet we will see more people "home, alone and anonymous." Specifically, the survey found that of those people who use the Internet from home five hours or more per week,

13 percent spend less time with family and friends, 8 percent attend fewer social events, 25 percent spend less time shopping in stores, and 25 percent are working more at home without any decline in work at the office.

Luba is certainly an excellent example of how Internet use, and its most common application, e-mail, allowed her to remain connected to work while at home. Even after working a twelve-hour day, Luba reports that she would often return home, heat up something in the microwave to eat quickly, and retreat to her study to e-mail coworkers about the day's project or to continue personal conversations upon which work had intruded. When I asked where her husband and children were at these times, she replied:

> "Oh, they were in their rooms too, probably online. We have five phone lines in our house, but my company paid for mine."

Did you miss talking to them, finding out about their day?
> "Yes, of course, but I would usually be pretty wired, you know, after working so hard. It would be hard to focus on anything else, but yes, I always wanted to know about my kids' day."

So how would you find out, find out about their day?
> "Oh, sometimes while we were getting breakfast and sometimes when it was my turn to take them to school."

Never in the evenings?
> "Oh, my kids are like their father. They like to be alone a lot. They're all involved in projects, you know for school, and for the things they're interested in. I mean maybe we should spend more time talking at night. I don't know."

In suggesting that her children, much like her husband, prefer to be alone, Luba seems to deny her own preoccupation with work as well as her children's adaptation to their parents' lifestyle. This kind of denial, however, is not unique to Luba. In her book *The Time Bind,* Arlie Hochschild discovered that the working parents she interviewed often denied their children's needs in order to avoid feeling guilty about the number of hours they spend at work:

> In the grip of a time bind, working parents redefine as nonessential more than a child's need for security and companionship. Pressed for time, many two-job couples I've studied questioned a variety of other kinds of familial needs. One husband told me, "We don't really need a hot meal at night because we eat well at lunch . . ." Yet another challenged the need for her children's daily baths or clean clothes: "He loves his brown pants. Why shouldn't he just wear them for a week . . ?" Of a three-month old child in nine-hour daycare, a father assured me, "I want him to be independent . . ."
>
> If, in the earlier part of the century, many middle-class children suffered from overattentive mothers, from being "mother's only accomplishment," many of today's children may suffer from a parental desire for reassurance that they are free of needs.

The Workday That Never Ends

If family life is increasingly characterized by isolation and the denial of emotional needs, what interests does it then serve?

From listening to my patients and from reading contemporary accounts of family life in the United States, it seems that, in many cases, the family is becoming more and more an extension of work. Clearly, it is work that determines family time: when we awaken, when we eat, when we are together, when we need childcare, when we can have fun, when we go to bed. In *The Working Life,* when Joanne Ciulla reminds us that the "clock and the schedule rob our social life of spontaneity," we can add that the workplace robs families of the ability to control time. While this has been true since the dawn of industrialization, the ways in which work invades and controls the home today is historically unique.

As we have seen, Americans are working more than ever before. The hours that were reserved for family—evenings, weekends, holidays—are being eroded by work, and this erosion is occurring rapidly. For example, in 1986, when Christmas fell on a Thursday, 46 percent of employers gave workers Friday off. In 1997, when Christmas next fell on a Thursday, only 36 percent did. Clearly, it is not only the hours spent on the job that allows work to determine family time. New forms of technology have radically altered many people's family life in just the past ten years.

In March 2000, the *New York Times* ran an article entitled, "For the Well Connected, All the World's an Office: Cell Phones, Pagers and Wireless E-Mail Have Created a Workday That Never Ends." In it, reporter Katie Hafner asserts that "Hyperconnectedness does not necessarily mean that people are going into the office less. More often than not, it means that when they leave the office, they keep at least part of their minds focused on work." To illustrate this phenomenon, Hafner describes Peter Huemer, a computer consultant who not only owns both a cell phone and a pager, but they are at his side every minute of every day. He also checks his e-mail compulsively.

Mr. Huemer knows that he no longer has a life outside work . . .

Dinners in restaurants, Ms. Huemer [his wife] said, are often marred by incoming cell phone calls. That leaves her to pick at her food, while her husband spends half an hour coaching someone through a computer problem.

Mr. Huemer is not unsympathetic to his wife's concerns. "She's unhappy about what she sees as a constant intrusion," he said. "I walk in the house and instead of saying hello, I have a phone on my ear."

So blurred has the line between work and home become that the Huemers are in marriage counseling. Mr. Huemer takes both cell phone and pager to his sessions. . . .

This kind of blurring certainly characterizes Luba's life. Bereft of e-mail, her time at home would have been different. Luba did not like to watch television, and prefers reading to TV. I asked her what she did before she had e-mail:

"Well, the kids were younger then so I had to spend more time there—giving them baths, reading to them, all that."

So e-mail changed the amount of time you spent with your kids.

"I can't say it was the e-mail per se, because they were younger. But I think it did change my preoccupations. I think [with e-mail] maybe it wasn't so easy to just forget about work when I got home, because I'd think 'well, I send so-and-so an e-mail about something that happened that day and maybe she'll be online and write back if I can send it to her early enough.' You know, that kind of thing."

"That kind of thing" nicely describes not only how work invades our preoccupations, our daydreams and emotional lives, but how electronic leashes facilitate that invasion and give it entrée into our homes, our presumed time away from our jobs. E-mail, cell phones, faxes, and pagers materially break down the boundary between home and work, and provide the means for us to transform our homes into auxiliary work stations. Dinesh D'Souza notes that, due to these technologies, "The sharp distinction between the home and the workplace, which is an artifact of the Industrial Revolution, is becoming blurred and might eventually be abolished."

In many ways, then, the family can be seen as a locus of coordination that enables us to work. In it, schedules, activities, and outsourcing can be coordinated. Typically, with mother as coordination manager, adults' work schedules and children's day-care and school schedules can be timed together. Who drives junior to day care; who picks him up; where he can stay when the day care center closes before his parents' work day ends; who goes to watch his older sister's piano recital; who can be found to babysit when the company's party occurs are all scheduling questions coordinated within the family. Activities from soccer to piano lessons to shopping for groceries and trips to the dentist need to be assigned and planned in advance. Of course, all of this revolves around hours set by work.

Outsourcing means that functions previously performed within families can be done by nonfamily for pay. Thus, child rearing, food preparation, household chores, and talking out problems together can be assigned to day-care centers, the *home-meal-replacement industry* (takeout, home delivery, online meal selection), franchised cleaning companies like Merry Maids, and psychotherapists.

Relatively new forms of outsourcing are springing up rapidly in response to the erosion of family life by work. Doggie day-care centers are opening to care for dogs that are alone for long hours while everyone works or is in child day care. Judith Kaufman, who helped open one of the first day care centers for dogs, comments: "This was a program that had to be started. When everyone in the family gets home at night, they are still too busy to play with the dog." Playground Connections, in Washington, DC, matches children with playmates. Grandma Please! is a 1-900 telephone number that children can call to reach an adult who will talk with them, sing to them, or help with homework. Honey Do is a Bay Area company that supplies handymen to come out to the home not only to perform household repairs, but to also change light bulbs and take out the garbage. Families can turn to babyproofing agencies, professional bill payers, household managers, and closet organizers to intervene, take charge, and mediate life within the home.

Outsourcing makes it easier for people to work, as it diminishes their household duties. It also, however, makes our homes into shells and our family lives feel empty. Joanne Ciulla observes that the "more the time demands of work dominate our lives, the more all activities feel like work." That seems exactly right. If most of our family meals are takeout; if more child rearing is done by paid professionals outside the home than by parents within it; if therapists are the only ones we turn to in distress; and even our dogs are eager to escape the loneliness of home, we have sacrificed family life in order to work. If reading a story to a child or preparing a family meal are viewed exclusively as tasks to get over with in order to recover from, or prepare for, our jobs, then it appears that work has triumphed over all.

LESS TO GO OUT TO

As family life is exerting less of an emotional and temporal pull on many of us, what about our neighborhoods and communities, those forms of embedded sociability that traditionally have lured us away from both work and home? Do they provide any kind of countervailing force to our enthrallment with our jobs?

Two case studies are particularly relevant here. I choose them because each confounded my own assumptions about neighborhood and community life in the contemporary American landscape. I thought both Grace and Jim, compared to many of my patients, might have access to a life outside both home and work that they could turn to in a time of need and that would be emotionally sustaining.

Grace, a forty-seven-year-old mother of three, grew up in the inner city, the only child of a single mother who worked as a cook during the day and a janitor at night. Grace dropped out of school at fifteen, had her first child at seventeen, and has worked at a variety of fairly menial jobs since that time. At present, she lives alone in a one-bedroom apartment. Her youngest child is twenty-three. Her one son is in prison. Grace hasn't heard from one of her daughters in years, after throwing her out of her house for refusing to give up drugs. Her other daughter joined the Navy and visits her mother whenever she has leave. Grace's own mother died some years ago, and she is not close to her aunts or cousins.

For the past nine years, Grace has worked as a clerk in a large discount supermarket. Her immediate supervisor, Tanya, is ten years younger than Grace, but someone whom Grace admires: "She has style, you know, and a sense of humor! That girl can think on her feet, always has a comeback, don't let anyone put her down." Grace feels that she and Tanya became good friends. Tanya often would call Grace at night, telling her her problems, asking for advice about how to handle employee issues at work. The two would occasionally take their lunch hours together, walking around a nearby park and gossiping about other employees. Grace felt that her coworkers envied her relationship with their mutual supervisor, Tanya.

Around the time Grace turned forty-six, she began experiencing some gynecological problems that caused her to repeatedly see her doctor. She had to have numerous tests, and, eventually, a hysterectomy was recommended. This frightened her because she had never had surgery, and made her anxious because her doctor could not assure her that the hysterectomy would absolutely eliminate the pain and bladder problems she was experiencing. However, none of the feelings about her health compared to Grace's disappointment about the seeming lack of concern Tanya showed for Grace's medical problems, and the lack of interest her coworkers evinced when hearing the details of her upcoming surgery. Each time Grace returned to work after a doctor's appointment, neither Tanya nor her coworkers said anything. In response, Grace became sullen and withholding. When Tanya would talk with Grace about other employees, Grace remained silent. She couldn't believe Tanya "cared about that stupid stuff when I was looking at surgery."

Grace's overall health began to decline. She was placed on blood-pressure medication and complained of pain and numbness in different parts of her body. Believing that Grace was overly concerned about the impending hysterectomy, her physician referred her for psychotherapy to help her cope better with her anxieties but, once in therapy with me, Grace spoke almost exclusively of Tanya and her coworkers. Each day at work seemed to bring yet another instance of someone's disregard for Grace's feelings. Although she could talk openly about her fears of surgery, these became the backdrop for the interpersonal saga that dominated Grace's feelings: "I thought they were my friends. I thought they cared."

Six weeks into our therapy, Grace returned to work from a doctor's appointment and met Tanya as she walked into the store. The first words out of her supervisor's mouth were a request for her to work overtime that evening. This was simply too much for Grace to bear. She turned away from Tanya, walked back to her car and drove home. She called me soon thereafter, crying, saying she could not return to work. Would I fill out forms for her to qualify for short-term disability because, "I'm no use to anyone anyway."

Unable to go to work, Grace isolated herself in her apartment and survived on the small amount of money she received every two weeks from California state disability. She did not tell her daughter in the Navy what had befallen her, because she felt this daughter had her own life, and didn't wish to burden her. Grace stated repeatedly that she felt she had no one with whom to share her feelings because all her friends were at the store and they had turned against her. None of her coworkers called, and Grace assumed that they had rallied around Tanya, and couldn't understand the emotional pain Grace was experiencing.

When I asked Grace about her extended family or about people in her neighborhood, she explained:

My mother always worked, but her people and my father's people [were] always on assistance. My mother taught me pride in myself. Her side of the family is pretty tight knit and some of them live pretty close by . . . Yeah, they see each other a lot. But, you see, my mother worked and I worked. We never did take part in their goin's on. I think the family was jealous. "You too good for us" kinda thing. Yeah I know my neighbors; I grew up with them, but it's the same thing with them, too. I always was at work and when I got home I took care of my babies. I don't like to associate too much there, you know. I think they're kinda jealous, too.

Grace's dedication to work set her apart from her family and community. Following her mother's example, Grace supported herself and her children, and this took her away from her neighborhood for long hours. Her pride in herself—as evinced through her work ethic—compelled her to eschew those around her who did not value work in the same way. Thus, for Grace, dedication to work and involvement in family and community were mutually exclusive.

On the surface, Jim's story is quite different from Grace's. Jim is a thirty-three-year-old advertising executive who came to therapy after being accused of mishandling a major advertising campaign. This, he tells me, is the first time in his life that he has experienced failure. Due to his movie-star good looks, quick wit, and engaging sense of humor, Jim has moved through life with seeming ease. Having grown up on Long Island in an upper-middle-class family, attending an Ivy League college, and having immediately been launched on a high-powered career in advertising, Jim assumed success. He has been involved in a number of relationships, but each of these took a back seat to Jim's involvement in work. "My sense was now's the time to build the career, sock away the money, and settle down later."

In an effort to "build the career," Jim often worked seven days per week. Some of this work was done telecommuting from the house Jim had bought at age twenty-nine in the Berkeley hills. This house was painstakingly decorated, and Jim's home office—filled with every possible high-tech accouterment—held a commanding view of the San Francisco Bay. His house and its furnishings were a "mirror of my success. Every time I walked in the door, I thought 'you have *made* it.'"

When things began turning sour at work, Jim increasingly retreated into his home, ostensibly spending more time telecommuting. In truth, he did little work and passed increasing amounts of time ruminating about his situation. He would stare out the window contemplating the meaning of life. At these moments, he would experience a profound sense of loneliness, a bone-cold emptiness that made him feel detached from everything around him. These periods of detachment are what prompted him to seek therapy. They made him feel as though he were losing his mind.

Jim first started seeing me once, then twice, then three times a week, in an effort to feel connected to someone. In these sessions, he began to realize how much he had used work to stave off feelings of emptiness and disconnection. He began to wonder aloud about whether knowing he was gay from an early age made him close himself off to others. He hypothesized that being successful covered over other feelings, feelings of being unbearably different from those around him:

It's funny, but I can't even imagine how I'd go about making a friend. In college or at work, people always found *me*. I never had to find *them*. I guess I went from high school to college to this job and it was always all right there. I never had to *do* anything to have a life; I just had one. Now I just feel adrift, at sea, you know? Unless you're into the bar scene, what do you do, where do you go?

It is this question: What do you do, where do you go? that I hear throughout my workday, repeated in various ways by virtually all of my patients, that is, all of my workplace exiles. Having annexed their lives to their jobs, they cannot imagine how to connect with others outside of work, how to find identity, purpose, or a sense of belonging that is not in some way structured by an employer.

This pervasive sense of disconnectedness apparently is part of a larger social trend in the United States today, evidenced in a variety of ways.

Socializing outside of work is declining. Based on his review of surveys from the last quarter century, Robert Putnam declares that "The pace of decline in social visiting over the last twenty-five years has been extraordinary." In the 1990s, Americans entertained friends at home about 45 percent less than they did in the 1970s, from fourteen or fifteen times a year to eight. "Entertaining, *c'est mort*," the *New York Times Magazine* declared in its November 5, 2000, edition. In that article, we discover that in "L.A., they don't go to dinner parties during the week for fear that someone might think they are not working." A survey of Americans' "readiness to make new friends" found a decrease of one-third between 1985/86 and 1998/99. In an article in the *Wall Street Journal,* reporter Nancy Ann Jeffrey asks:

Didn't we used to have friends? Everyone from high-level executives to stay-at-home moms seems to have the same complaint these days: People just don't put the same priority on friendship anymore. Blame it on longer hours at work, soaring business travel and the flood of infotainment that keeps us wired to just about everything but other people . . .

The marginalization of friendship is a historical anomaly . . . In America, [friendship] has been a staple of popular culture from bridge clubs to buddy movies. Not anymore: The early '90s kaffeeklatsches on "Friends" and "Seinfeld" have given way to shows about teen angst and various ways to become a millionaire.

Between 1974 and 1998, the frequency with which Americans "spend a social evening with someone who lives in your neighborhood" declined by about one-third. Compared with the 1950s, the decline is about one-half.

While socializing outside work decreases, so does community participation in face-to-face volunteer organizations. Involvement in all kinds of groups—from fraternal organizations to garden clubs, PTAs, and church groups—is dramatically down. According to Putnam, "In the ten short years between 1985 and 1994, active involvement in community organizations in this country fell by 45 percent. By this measure, at least, nearly half of America's civic infrastructure was obliterated in barely a decade."

Undoubtedly, women's steadily increasing labor-force participation accounts for a good part of this change. Historically, it has been women's unpaid labor that has cemented ties among neighbors, provided the backbone of volunteer organizations and community groups, raised the money, run the bake sales, provided succor to those in need. Thirty years ago, stay-at-home moms knit communities together, and provided their families with a place within their neighborhoods. Today, they work. Their houses remain empty throughout the day. There are no kaffeeklatsches or gossiping over the fence. Neighborhoods stand lifeless, as men and women alike now toil at work during the week and run errands and collapse in front of the television on the weekend.

This lack of social connectedness is also reflected in the declining frequency with which both married and single people frequent bars, nightclubs, discos, and taverns, that is, places where we might encounter neighbors, people from our communities, and strangers. Over the last two decades, spending time in these kinds of establishments has fallen by 40 to 50 percent. Simultaneously, between 1970 and 1998, the number of full-service restaurants decreased by one-quarter, and the number of bars and luncheonettes declined by one-half. During the same period, the number of fast-food outlets doubled. These changes prompt Robert Putnam to comment that unlike "the 'regulars' at the local bar or café, few of the other people waiting impatiently at McDonald's are likely to know your name or even to care that they don't . . . In effect, Americans have increasingly chosen to grab a bite and run rather than sit a while and chat."

With the decline of volunteerism, civic participation, and the frequenting of local restaurants and bars, Americans lose contact with their neighbors and with their communities. We lose our ability to know how to connect with others outside a structured work environment. We are less ready to make new friends, perhaps, in part, because we are losing our confidence, our facility for knowing how to encounter others and feel comfortable around them when they are not coworkers, managers, or supervisees. The way in which most of us increasingly engage with others outside the home or office is as faceless passersby in chain-dominated malls. Shopping has become the one thing that seems to consistently draw us into public space. However, we shop not to encounter the other or to be known. We shop to be in the presence of others as we admire and acquire things.

As our interest in engaging with others diminishes, knowing how to spend time outside work, how to have leisure, is thwarted. In his thoughtful essay, "The Fall of Fun," James Atlas bemoans a society in which work and an ethos of productivity has enfeebled our "openness to experience," our willingness to do "something just for the hell of it," "the inconsequential hours that gave life its accidental charm: when was the last time a friend just dropped by and stayed for dinner?"

Sociologist Arlie Hochschild echoes this lament when she asserts that, as we give more of our lives to our jobs, we are becoming "emotional ascetics." While she specifically focuses on the ways in which we steel ourselves "against both the need to care for others and the need to be cared for" as we spend longer hours at work, I think emotional asceticism increasingly pervades our lives in general. We make do with less—less time, less fun, less attention, less understanding, less intimacy, and certainly less care. We do not expect to know our neighbors or to be recognized by others when we walk into a local store. We do not assume we can drop over to a friend's house unannounced. We berate ourselves for not accomplishing all that is on our to-do list on the weekends. We do not feel we deserve time to do nothing, to not be productive. Acting spontaneously and having fun go against the grain of our work-obsessed culture. Many of us even have difficulty allowing our *children* to play, when they could be learning, taking lessons, preparing for their future lives as workers. Leisure is now defined by how "hard" we are in its pursuit: "work hard, play hard." Spending a Sunday in bed—reading, making love, reflecting on one's life—are too soft, too indulgent, too unproductive, when we could be taking a class on mutual-fund investing, training for a marathon, or catching up on e-mail.

Family and community began to dissolve in the 1960s and 1970s, in part due to a desire in our culture for greater personal freedom, individual expression and self-fulfillment. In response to the cultural constraints of the 1950s, many Americans shared a collective desire to break the ties that bound men to monotonous, unfulfilling work, and women to lives of stifling domesticity. A quest for libidinous experimentation, individual creativity, leisure, and questioning authority in all forms propelled people to leave expectations and obligations behind. Somehow, over the course of the last thirty years, that desire has been thwarted as we all—men and women alike—are more tethered to work than ever before. We may have exchanged gray-flannel suits for t-shirts and jeans, but we have allowed our jobs to harness our desires and utilize them for the greater good of the corporation. Personal freedom has been redefined as the freedom to change jobs, self-fulfillment as success at work. Libidinous self-expression has been sublimated into the twelve-hour day, often punctuated by visits to pornography websites or brief encounters. We are a nation of emotional ascetics, for whom personal productivity repudiates leisure, fun, and the need to care for others and be cared for. Rather than being self-indulgent, increasing numbers of Americans appear to deny many of their needs and desires. We may surround ourselves with relatively lavish commodities, but we quietly put up with a remarkable level of aloneness and emptiness outside our jobs.

It is this tolerance for being alone in the world, and having diminished expectations for the care, attention, and support they might receive that so deeply colors my patients' lives. Bereft of work, they literally do not know what to do with themselves. Most spend their days watching television, often too filled with shame to venture beyond the front door. "Everybody in my building works," Marion reports. "I don't want anybody to know I can't work, so I keep the drapes closed all day." Lionel also stays home watching television while his wife and stepson work. "Where would I go? Everybody works, and if you don't work, something's wrong with you." Like so many of my patients, Luba feels that she cannot turn to others for support during this crisis because "This is *my* problem. I need to just get over it. Other people can't understand what it's like." For so many of the patients I see, I, a paid professional, constitute their main emotional support. Through their eyes everyone works, has his or her own problems, is too busy to have the time or inclination to care. *And this is just the way it is,* they tell me over and over. There is no sense of surprise or outrage or grief over their being alone with their problems. To not feel deeply connected to their families or communities, to not know what to do with themselves outside of work aside from watch television, to not know how to have fun, are facts that are both expected and assumed. This is, I would suggest, a far cry from what personal freedom is supposed to be.

With the decline of family, neighborhood, and community, we become a "society without institutional shelters," according to author Richard Sennett. Not only do we have less to come home to and less to go out to, we have less of a means for anchoring our selves and evaluating our circumstances and experiences. As we live more of our lives outside of institutional shelters where we are long-term witnesses to each other's lives, where we experience a shared history and a collective memory, we lack reference points for understanding ourselves and what goes on around us. In this denuded landscape, the workplace can seem like one's only mooring, providing emotional shelter, meaning, and direction.

CHAPTER THREE

The Glue That Holds the Self Together

MICHELLE AND I HAD BEEN MEETING in once-per-week psychotherapy for almost a year. An attorney had referred the twenty-six-year-old administrative assistant to me after she approached him about filing a sexual harassment suit against her employer. Apparently, when Michelle met with this lawyer for a consultation, she broke down, sobbing, in his office and couldn't control herself enough to tell him what had happened. So, he sent her to me.

Michelle was a very attractive, extremely gentle young woman who seemed somewhat bewildered by her plight. She had taken a job as the assistant to the owner of an import–export business in San Francisco when she was twenty-four. She says that she "loved" her job; the company; her boss, Glenn; and the other employees. She states that they "were like a family," and that she happily worked extra hours and "helped out" in ways that certainly exceeded her job description. Without any self-consciousness or embarrassment, Michelle told me that she had been dissatisfied with the janitorial service her company employed, so she routinely—and secretly—cleaned the bathrooms herself after hours. Occasionally, she brought in her vacuum cleaner and cleaned the carpets. She also was an excellent cook and frequently baked goodies on Sunday night to share with her boss and coworkers on Monday.

By her own description, Michelle looked up to Glenn, and felt particularly good about herself whenever he praised her for a job well done. He had started the company on his own some twelve years earlier, and Michelle was extremely impressed at how successful he had been. After many months in therapy, Michelle could admit that she increasingly did things to impress this man and would beat herself up when he hadn't noticed her extra efforts. "I would just think you know that I maybe was to blame; I hadn't done something right, and I'd try to think what I could do better, get him to notice."

Given her respect, perhaps even adoration, for him, Michelle was thrilled when Glenn told her he'd like to take her out to lunch for National Secretaries Day. In anticipation of this lunch, Michelle bought a new outfit and spent an unusual amount of time doing her hair and applying makeup before going to work on the day they were to have lunch. In retrospect, Michelle wonders about how much makeup she put on and how low cut her blouse was: "I know I wanted to impress him. I don't know what I was thinking . . . I guess I wasn't really thinking. I just wanted, I don't know something . . . Maybe to be noticed. Well to have him like me, definitely . . . I had this Wonder Bra that I wore on weekends but never to work. But this was a special occasion and so I thought 'why not?'"

Michelle describes feeling almost ecstatic as she sat in her boss's Lexus on the way to lunch. Glenn was regaling her with stories of what had just happened at a meeting he had with a company he was thinking of acquiring. "I couldn't really believe he was telling me all this. He swore me to secrecy. And I thought, God, he really must think a lot of me, I mean, really trust me." They went to a restaurant on the bay with a view of the Bay Bridge and proceeded to drink margaritas. Her boss talked about business throughout the lunch, telling her his plans for expandimg the company. By her second margarita, Michelle couldn't really follow what he was saying but nevertheless felt honored and excited that he was talking to her in this way.

Michelle explains that this mode of conversation continued in the car on the ride back to work, as they walked down the hall to his office and as he closed the door behind them. Then, suddenly, Glenn turned around and pinned Michelle against the wall, kissing her deeply and fondling her breasts. Michelle states "I went into fight or flight," and she struggled to get him off her. Somehow her silk blouse tore as she pushed him away and ran out of the office. Breathless, with her blouse torn and smudged mascara encircling her eyes, Michelle found herself face to face with Susan, the office manager, a woman in her fifties whom Michelle respected and baked lemon bars for. Michelle has a difficult time reconstructing exactly what happened next, because she became "hysterical." She couldn't stop crying and shaking. Susan took her home and they sat together on Michelle's bed for almost an hour going over what had happened and trying to figure out what to do. Susan was adamant that Michelle should file a sexual-harassment suit against Glenn after informing her that she was aware of at least two other incidents in which Glenn had made unwanted sexual advances against female employees.

Unable to return to work out of embarrassment, fear, and simply bewilderment, Michelle contacted an attorney recommended by Susan, and then was referred to me.

For almost a year, Michelle and I talked about what had happened at her office, how her eagerness to please, her longing for recognition, and her naiveté had made her vulnerable to Glenn. Without condoning her boss's behavior or blaming Michelle for his attack, we examined the needs and longings she brought to the workplace, and the ways in which these could never be appropriately satisfied at a job. Michelle remained off work on Workers' Compensation disability for a number of months, and then decided to look for a new job. I believed she had made a good amount of progress and was pleased that she wished to continue our work together even after finding new employment. I therefore was startled at our meeting following her first day at her new job.

Michelle had been hired at a large corporation in Silicon Valley. She had been interviewed off site, and was astounded on her first day of work at the corporation's headquarters. Her first view of her new company was of the three-story-high slide that dominated the lobby. The employees wore t-shirts, jeans, and shorts. She was told that she could drop off clothes that needed to be dry cleaned with the receptionist for her team, who would have them returned to her by the end of the following day. There was not only free coffee available but Cokes, mineral waters, and jelly beans. Most impressive to her, however, was her new supervisor, Shelby, a twenty-seven-year-old graduate of Brown University, who greeted her new administrative assistant wearing a Brown University sweatshirt, shorts, and hiking boots. Shelby sat on Michelle's desk telling her that they worked for the "best company in the valley," and shared with Michelle the story of her own meteoric rise to assistant vice president at the age of twenty-six. Shelby told Michelle that by joining the company, she was now "home free."

When Michelle entered my office she was transported, mesmerized by her new employer. She couldn't stop talking about her supervisor, how everything Shelby did was an inspiration and worthy of being emulated. Michelle's only desire was to live up to Shelby's expectations and not let her down. When I tried to gently remind Michelle of what we had worked on together over the past months, of how her feelings about Shelby bore a striking resemblance to those she had evinced toward Glenn, Michelle insisted that this was altogether different. Because Shelby was a woman, and because this huge corporation was so vastly different from her previous employer, there could be no comparison. Over the course of the next few weeks, when I would refer to our previous conversations and attempt to look at the similarities in her approach to work, Michelle would assume a tone of beleaguered condescension: "Maybe if you were there, you'd see . . . It's like Shelby said, I'm home free."

"Home free," I'd find myself repeating silently to myself. So Michelle is now *home free*. What does this mean?

- She's arrived
- She's arrived home
- Work is freeing
- Work is home
- Work is home that is freeing (in that you get to wear shorts, eat jelly beans supplied by the company, and play on a slide accompanied by your twenty-seven-year-old supervisor)

As our sessions continued, all efforts on my part to engage Michelle in questioning her idealization of her supervisor and new employer failed. Michelle had again annexed herself to her job. She stayed late virtually every day, in a neverending attempt to earn Shelby's approval and praise. She provided home-baked pastries so often that her coworkers began putting in orders for their favorites. To satisfy these requests, Michelle began her baking earlier and earlier, often spending most of her Sundays in her kitchen. After three months at this job, Michelle told me that her team was more like a family to her than her own family had been. Two weeks later, Michelle left a message on my voice mail informing me that she could no longer come to therapy because our 6:30 meetings on Wednesday evenings interfered with her ability to stay late at work. When I tried to reach her to discuss this decision, she chose not to return my calls.

It seems that my voice was simply too insignificant compared to the siren call of Michelle's workplace. For it was there that she found recognition, a sense of belonging, a chance to be acknowledged, and to be close to someone she deeply admired and idealized. Her new workplace provided her with esteem for both her clerical skills and her baking. It was family. And all the longings and needs and emotional hunger that resided in Michelle could be brought to that office building with a three-story slide and be responded to with the utterance that she was *home free*.

Yet, how do we explain Michelle?

RELATIONSHIPS AS OXYGEN

Throughout most of the twentieth century, our standards of both mental health and maturity were defined through the achievement of autonomous selfhood. Virtually all theories of psychological development were founded on a view of progress through clearly definable stages—from helpless dependency or symbiosis with one's mother, to full independence or autonomy. The specifics of the stages that one mastered in between may have had different foci—Freud's oral, anal, and oedipal; Margaret Mahler's separation–individuation and rapprochement; Erik Erikson's trust versus mistrust, autonomy versus shame and doubt, and initiative versus guilt. But all of them ended in the apotheosis of maturity as autonomy from others.

In the past few decades, theories of human development have begun to shift. Informed by theoretical advances in developmental psychology, psychoanalysis, and feminism, mature adulthood is being redefined as a state of being that is intrinsically dependent on ties to a sustaining and reliable environment of other people. Rather than viewing our need to feel connected to others as a sign of weakness or immaturity, *mature dependence* or *self-in-relationship* are increasingly accepted as definitions of mental health and maturity. Psychoanalyst Heinz Kohut, one of the leading theorists of this shift in thinking, has stated that relationships with others that are both present in our everyday lives and internalized within our psyches "form the essence of psychological life from birth to death. . . ."

> [A] move from dependence (symbiosis) to independence (autonomy) in the psychological sphere is no more possible, let alone desirable, than a corresponding move from a life dependent on oxygen to a life independent of it in the biological sphere.

Stephen Mitchell, another psychoanalytic theorist who has been instrumental in altering our understanding of human development and mental health in adulthood, writes:

There is no "self" in a psychologically meaningful sense, in isolation, outside a matrix of relations with others . . .

The process involved in the preservation of one's personal psychological world might be compared to the factors involved in maintaining the structural cohesion of the human body . . . Ties to others, like the bones, are often not visible to the naked eye but provide an underlying skeletal framework which holds experience together. In order to maintain a "stable, coherent sense of self" we need "dependable, sustaining connections with others."

Kohut uses the term *selfobjects* to denote others whom we use to evoke, maintain, or enhance our sense of self. In order to be human, and to have a cohesive sense of self that endures over time, all of us need meaningful relationships with other people. These important others, these selfobjects, mirror back to us who we are and what we have of value. It is through our connection with them that we can feel secure and perhaps even significant or powerful if we imbue them with authority and stature. However, it is critical to understand from a psychological perspective that selfobjects do not exist for us merely on an interpersonal level, but on intrapsychic and intersubjective levels as well. What I mean by this is that we take them into our psyches, where they operate both consciously and unconsciously, where they become part of who we are, operating on an *intrapsychic* level. This taking in, or internalization, is never complete, however. We do not take these relationships in and then exist independently of them. We need their presence in our environment to reaffirm and sustain the selfobject functions we have internalized; thus they operate on an *intersubjective* level, as well.

For Michelle, her bosses, first Glenn, then Shelby, served important selfobject functions. Because she idealized them both, being connected to them, being acknowledged and liked by them, made Michelle feel good about herself not only when she was around them. Michelle partially internalized their recognition of her so that she could wake up in the morning feeling strong and secure, without consciously thinking of them. She could spend her Sundays baking, and be content without consciously imagining the reception her baked goods would receive. Because her supervisor's—and, to a lesser degree, coworkers'—positive regard for her lived inside her, Michelle could feel worthwhile simply by engaging in an activity that was associated with eliciting that regard.

But she used these selfobjects in her idiosyncratic, time-honored ways. She continued to feel that the important people at work accepted and cared for her because of what she did—the extra efforts she made around the office, the cookies she baked, the compliments she routinely bestowed. Because her supervisors and coworkers were not Michelle's therapist, mentor, or true friends, they readily participated in her enactment of trying to please in order to be liked. They appreciated her for what she did for them or for the company.

Thus, when Michelle left her job because of Glenn's sexual affront, no one from the office called her, no one seemed to care about what had happened to her. After Susan's initial help, Michelle never heard from her again. This total disregard reconfirmed Michelle's worst suspicions: that she is only acceptable or valuable to others if she is constantly tending to their needs. She has no intrinsic value for who she is. Whatever self-esteem or value she had internalized from being connected to Glenn and her coworkers did not adhere in the face of her leaving the company. In reality, her relationship to him and others at work was not dependable or sustaining, but contingent and thereby faulty. As psychoanalyst Howard Bacal asserts:

> Without this selfobject experience, one loses one's sense of well-being. When the selfobject experience is faulty, the sense of self gets lost, the self falls apart, fragmentation or regression occurs—however one wants to express it. The selfobject experience is the glue that holds the self together.

Individuals are not created equal in their need as adults for selfobjects. The ways in which we are raised greatly influence how we approach our social environment, how hungry we are for recognition, esteem, and feelings of security from others. If we grow up surrounded by caregivers who are empathic and consistent, we can develop a sense of self that is relatively resilient and stable. We can move freely, as Stephen Mitchell asserts, "between attachment and self-definition, and between connection and differentiation." Our ongoing need for others is defined and modulated by a cohesive sense of who we are that endures over time. That sense of self is supported, enriched, and sustained by our connections with significant others. That sense can be disrupted and challenged when we are betrayed by selfobjects whom we rely on as adults.

If, however, our childhoods are not based on relationships with empathic, nurturing, and attuned caregivers, we can develop a sense of self that is unstable, fragmented, and/or in constant need of being propped up and supported. Rather than using selfobjects in our environment to mirror back to us our already established identities and self-esteem, we may need to depend on others to *provide us* with a sense of who we are and of our value as individuals. In the absence of a cohesive self that is felt to be worthy of recognition, valuation, and love, we can constantly attempt to seek out selfobjects in our environment who will provide us with those feelings and experiences that have never taken root within. Thus, we approach the world with tremendous hunger: hunger to be acknowledged, accepted, admired and praised, valued and loved.

Often such hunger can truly be satisfied in adulthood. Increasingly, psychotherapy is founded on this recognition. By providing a caring, consistent, and long-term relationship in which a patient is truly seen and empathized with, a therapist can facilitate the development of a cohesive sense of self and true self-esteem in his or her patient. Likewise, enduring, close relationships—with an intimate partner, best friend, or mentor—can provide a valued sense of self that might not have cohered in childhood due to failures in early caregiving relationships.

In truth, all of us probably exist somewhere along a continuum of selfobject need. Even those of us who experienced truly excellent care as children have our vulnerabilities and, therefore, turn to others in adulthood to help us cope with them. People's needs for selfobjects seem to range from wanting and aiming for others to acknowledge and value the self, to craving and desperately searching for others to prop up a self that lacks solidity. Many of us probably have an admixture of these states at any one time, and/or we experience different states of selfobject hunger across our life. For instance, adolescence is a time in which the need for others to help consolidate the self and form identity is particularly powerful.

From a psychological perspective, I believe that one way of understanding how my patients end up married to their jobs is through discerning their selfobject needs: With what kind or degree of emotional hunger and longing do they approach the workplace at this point in their lives? How much do they rely on others to provide them with a sense of who they are, of their value as individuals? Does their sense of self cohere over time, or is it contingent on what they do, who they know, how they are received by others?

It is my sense that most of my patients who marry their jobs have an extreme form of selfobject hunger. They look to relationships at work to prop up the self, to feel recognized, valued, and even, at times, loved. To use Stephen Mitchell's metaphor, their bones are weak. The glue that holds the self together hasn't adhered or isn't uniformly applied.

Michelle is a case in point. She describes a childhood in which she always felt shy and insecure. She believes that her parents were always too busy to spend much time with her and favored her younger sister who, virtually from birth, seemed more outgoing and sure of herself than Michelle. Elementary school was an ordeal, in that she experienced herself as completely unsuccessful at making friends, doing well academically, or participating in athletics. Things began to change for her, however, when she entered puberty. Michelle blossomed into a very attractive young woman and began to garner male attention. This, she feels, gave her a greater cachet with the other girls, and she became popular. Underlying her popularity, however, was always the feeling that, if people really got to know her, if they could see behind her attractive appearance, they would reject her. So, Michelle dedicated herself to pleasing others. If she constantly worked to take care of those she admired and wished to impress, she would be accepted and loved. If she stopped, people would see her for what she was: unlovable, inadequate.

Brenda, I think, employed an unconscious strategy similar to Michelle's. A childhood characterized by what Brenda felt was parental indifference and, at times, neglect, left her craving figures of authority who could acknowledge and value her. By being connected to people she admired and idealized she felt secure. At her law firm, Brenda felt she had arrived, much in the same way as Michelle had after meeting Shelby.

Ingrid and Luba seem to have more circumscribed selfobject needs than Michelle and Brenda. Ingrid grew up in a family that emphasized being productive as the ultimate measure of a worthy life. From early on, she internalized a belief that to be accepted she had to perform well. She could never just *be;* she had to *do.* The high-tech industry that she entered in her twenties fostered and exacerbated this unconscious belief. Her need for others to recognize her achievements was the selfobject glue that, in part, kept her working up to 110 hours per week.

Luba had a somewhat different need. Both within her family and among her peers, she always had been recognized as being an extremely intelligent, competent, and independent person. Her mother often claimed that Luba "knew what she wanted from the day she was born." Even though she could take pride in her self-direction and accomplishments, she felt that she never truly fit in or belonged. She believed her intelligence had set her apart from both her family and her classmates in the town in which she grew up in Eastern Europe. Thus, when Luba entered her new employer's campus on her first day of work, she was not unconsciously yearning for anyone to mirror back to her that she was valuable or worthy. She knew this in her bones. Rather, she wanted to fit in, to feel that she was acceptable to her peers. Because of this, she actually loved the fact that she wasn't considered in any way exceptional because of her intelligence or competence at her job. Everyone in her work group could be so characterized, thus allowing Luba to experience a profound and longed-for sense of belonging.

When my patients' unconscious needs are examined in this fashion, a crucial component of why they end up marrying their jobs is illuminated, but it does not tell us the whole story. For what we need to understand is not merely why particular individuals overinvest emotionally in their workplaces, but why such overinvestment appears to be a social trend, the new American way of life.

ATTENTION DEFICIT

As outlined in chapter 2, the steady decrease of institutional shelters in our society often leaves us without a sense of being anchored in a particular place, among a stable group of people, with a specified function or role. We move, change jobs, live with someone, break up, change friends, move, marry, have children, divorce, move, and so on. As psychologist Kenneth Gergen has pointed out:

> To the extent that one is surrounded by a cast of others who respond to one in a similar way, a sense of unified self may result.... However ... one now becomes transient, a nomad or a "homeless mind." The continuous reminders of one's identity—of who one is and always has been—no longer prevail....
>
> It is not only a coherent community that lends itself to the sense of personal depth. It is also the availability of others who provide the time and attention necessary for a sense of

an unfolding interior to emerge. . . . [O]ne acquires the sense
of depth primarily when there is ample time for exploration,
time for moving beyond instrumental calculations to matters of "deeper desire," forgotten fantasies, to "what really
counts." Yet, it is precisely this kind of "time off the merry-
go-round" that is increasingly difficult to locate.

Without using the terminology, it seems to me that Gergen
is echoing those psychoanalysts who speak of a lifelong need
for selfobjects. He then goes further, however, and makes a
particular historical and social argument, pointing out the diminished opportunities we now have for selfobject experience.
It is in family, neighborhood, and community that Americans
traditionally have been able to connect with "others who provide the time and attention necessary for a sense of an unfolding interior," or a coherent sense of self, to emerge. As those
institutions decline, we find ourselves making do with less time
and less attention from others. We become the "emotional ascetics" that Arlie Hochschild describes. And, as we do so, our
sense of who we are, the cohesiveness of our selves, becomes
precarious and depleted. Our lifelong need for selfobjects becomes more problematic. Increasingly, locating significant others who provide us with time for exploration, time that is not
measured, is a search that is arduous and haphazard. Often,
our neighbors do not know us; we have little time to see our
friends; the attention we get from others is piecemeal, hurried,
and certainly without the leisurely time for the exploration that
Gergen invokes.

All too many of us are suffering from an attention deficit.
As we work more, we have less time, less opportunity to attend
to each other's needs. As we suffer from this deficit, this ab-

sence of recognition and care in our personal lives, many of us find ourselves working more in order to escape or deny that absence, and to search for the attention we miss. If we cannot locate security and long-term connection—a cast of others who respond to one in a similar way—in the institutional shelters outside work, then perhaps we can make the workplace satisfy our selfobject needs.

I believe that this search for attention, care, and emotional resonance in the workplace is reflected in various studies of employee attitudes. The Hudson Institute issued a *1999 Employee Relationship Report Benchmark* study that found the six most important factors that determined employee commitment to work. In order of importance were 1) fairness, 2) care and concern for employees, 3) satisfaction with day-to-day activities, 4) trust in employees, 5) the reputation of the organization they worked for, and last, 6) the actual work and job resources. Clearly, relationships at work, and the way in which a company treats its employees, seem to be more important than the work in which individuals are actually engaged.

A metaanalysis of one million American workers conducted by the Gallup Organization underscores this even further:

> The single most important variable in employee productivity and loyalty turns out to be not pay or perks or benefits or workplace environment. Rather, according to the Gallup Organization, it's the quality of the relationship between employees and their direct supervisors. More specifically, what people want most from their supervisors is the same thing that kids want most from their parents: someone who sets clear and consistent expectations, cares for them, values their unique qualities, and encourages and supports their

growth and development. Put another way, *the greatest sources of satisfaction in the workplace are internal and emotional* (emphasis added).

Having met with close to two hundred patients to discuss issues about work, I would agree that the relationship with a supervisor is the most commonly discussed and emotionally fraught problem facing people who are married to their jobs. It is what propelled Brenda, Lionel, Sarah, Grace, and Michelle to see me. And, it is often the feeling that a supervisor doesn't care that is the most searing, the greatest betrayal. For what seems unbearable is not dislike but indifference, the feeling that we simply do not matter to someone whom we esteem.

I think this is understandable in light of people's selfobject hunger. For it is in the relationship with a supervisor that one is most apt to look for mirroring of the self and recognition that one is good and valuable. If we idealize our supervisors—as Brenda, Grace, and Michelle did—we can feel enriched, perhaps even empowered, by our connection to someone whom we imbue with authority and power.

Marion's story is a case in point. Marion, briefly referred to in chapter 2, had weathered a number of traumas before changing her life and becoming an account manager for Phaeton, a managed health-care organization. She had been sexually abused as a child, raped as a teenager, and began a serious drug addiction at age fifteen. Through sheer willpower she had entered drug rehabilitation, earned a B.A., and raised two daughters on her own. Marion clearly was a remarkably strong woman, yet she was also vulnerable in ways that were extremely difficult for her to acknowledge to herself or to others. She craved recognition from people she admired, and longed to be taken care of—something she could never fully accept in herself. These selfobject needs manifested themselves very dramatically and poignantly with Bill, Marion's supervisor.

Bill was a senior vice president of Phaeton and had supervised Marion for three years. He often talked about Phaeton as "one big family," which Marion found both apt and compelling (given her attraction to sentimental depictions of family life, reflected in her love of the *Godfather* movies). A fifty-eight-year-old father of five, Bill struck Marion as an extremely ethical, fair-minded man to whom she often turned for advice about problems at work. Although she did not believe that Bill favored her, she did think he respected her, and always was extremely laudatory in his evaluations of her. Because she admired Bill and trusted his judgment so completely, Marion made him the executor of her will. "He sort of reminded me of Marcus Welby. When he was around, you knew things were going to be okay."

After three years of feeling good about herself, her job, and her future, Marion became increasingly upset about a new director of operations who began to alter the way in which the account managers interfaced with clients. She voiced her concerns to Bill, and was surprised that, rather than welcoming the feedback, he seemed annoyed. Gradually, her supervisor's calm, benevolent mien changed. He became more critical and sharp. As Bill's attitude altered, Marion's ability to perform her job began to suffer. She often stayed after work trying to make up for her lack of concentration during the day. She increasingly got headaches, and began seeing her doctor for what was later diagnosed as irritable bowel syndrome. When Bill asked her for a report she had not completed, she states that she felt herself "sinking. It was like my identity was being taken away. I could tell he thought I was a fuckup."

Finally, Bill came into Marion's office holding in his hand a report she had submitted the previous day. She knew it was inadequate but was astounded at Bill's red face. "Are you the person for this job? Are you the person for this job?" she reports he shouted at her. He threw the report on her desk and stormed out the door. "That was it; I knew that was it. It was over." Marion sank into a vegetative depression that virtually rendered her mute, without connection to the world and without hope.

What exactly was over for Marion? Why was she unable to speak, unable to interact with others, even her daughters? Why did Bill's change in attitude seem to penetrate to the core of Marion's being?

I believe that, as she sat at her desk, blankly staring at the crumpled report, she was not calculating being fired and the attendant loss of wages, nor was she bemoaning her now diminished future capacity to consume, as many observers of the contemporary workplace would perhaps suggest. Rather, I think Marion experienced a profound loss of connection to a highly valued and much-needed selfobject. Her relationship to Bill had made her feel more secure than she had ever felt in her life. His understated, calm, and consistent acceptance and approval of Marion, allowed her sense of self to cohere and, to some degree, allowed her to feel valuable. He provided the much needed glue to hold her self together. And, given that her relationship to Bill was embedded within the "one big family" of Phaeton, Marion's need to feel a sense of belonging, of being part of a larger whole that seemed permanent and prestigious, was powerfully met. Bill provided Marion with a pervasive sense that things were going to be okay. Working at Phaeton gave her an identity.

In our first meeting, the centrality of Marion's workplace to her sense of self was palpable. She entered my office wearing a baseball cap, sweatshirt, and jeans. On both the cap and the sweatshirt was embroidered the word Phaeton. As she told me her story of profound betrayal and loss in a barely audible voice, I had the strangely uncomfortable feeling that I was talking to a person who had lost her tribe, or who was here on earth separated from her home planet. She still wore the clothes of that lost tribe, but she was in this world utterly alone. To conjure up the last remnants of identity with her people, she wore the clothes that signaled to me and to the world that she was a Phaeton.

This poignant attempt to maintain identity in the face of betrayal culminated in Marion's last gesture as she walked out my door. Having ended the session and scheduled a follow-up appointment, Marion handed me her Phaeton business card. In a strained voice she whispered, "This is who I was."

The drama of Marion's experience echoes throughout today's workplaces in diluted forms. Sharon, the chief financial officer of a corporation traded on the New York Stock Exchange, came to psychotherapy because she felt "too much of me is wrapped up in my job." After many sessions, largely conducted on the phone because she travels so much for work, Sharon revealed to me that her feelings of self-worth were dependent on her CEO's mood: "If Bernie is feeling good, I feel good. If he's down—and I can read that in a split second—I get down." Having understood that, I could see that Sharon tended to ruminate about her job, work longer hours, and ignore her personal life, when she perceived Bernie to be unhappy.

Lowell, the director of a large nonprofit corporation in San Francisco, joked with me in a psychotherapy session that together we should found a twelve-step group for "executives who care too much." Lowell's sense of himself and how valuable he is has revolved around the quarterly meetings he has with his board of directors. He describes entering these meetings with almost unbearable anticipation. If board members greet him with open, smiling faces, he feels "Relieved, no, more than relieved. It's more like a sense that I'm okay, who I am is okay." If, however, any of the members look critical, less than happy to see him, Lowell's sense of himself fades. "You can't imagine what it's like giving a quarterly report and feeling like you shouldn't be there, that you're a fake and they don't really want you."

Cynthia, a tenured professor at a local university, came to therapy after a close friend confronted her with how much she talks about her department. This friend warned her that, "If you spent that much time talking about a man, none of your friends would put up with it. They'd say to themselves: 'This woman calls herself a feminist?'" In our first session, Cynthia was clear about her motivations: "At age fifty, I realized I was never going to get married, never going to have a family. So, I think I made a conscious decision to just throw myself into that department, to make it like a family. And, I guess, now it's become my life." Although Cynthia has published a number of highly regarded books, has numerous mentoring relationships with graduate students, and enjoys many friendships with other academics, she lives in terror of retirement at age sixty-five. "It is simply unimaginable that I will not be going to the [weekly] departmental meeting," she states flatly. Cynthia's selfobject need for her department mirrors Brenda's psychological reliance on her law firm and that of Marion on Phaeton. Virtually no one, however, views Cynthia as emotionally needy or vulnerable. Her successful professional career, and the security of employment she has enjoyed through being tenured, have concealed the ways Cynthia uses her job to keep her sense of self glued together.

All That Is Solid Melts into Air

All fixed, fast-frozen relations, with their train of ancient and venerable prejudices and opinions, are swept away, all new-formed ones become antiquated before they can ossify. All that is solid melts into air.

—Karl Marx

As many people turn to their workplaces with unmet selfobject needs and, in turn, marry their jobs, most jobs do not offer the lifelong commitment that Cynthia experiences as a tenured professor. Corporations increasingly offer serial monogamy at best and one-night stands, at worst, to their employees. No longer is it 'til death do us part, but, rather, only as long as the task at hand shall last. As author Jerald Wallulis points out, the old economy was

> based on a "parental model" because it "offered to take care" of the employee, as long as the employee performed up to expectations. Under the new contract regime, company and employee are both adults who, as self governing units, contract with one another for their mutual benefit.

For many in our society, this new approach has been liberating. For those with high self-confidence, creativity, a capacity for, and joy in, working autonomously and with minimal constraint, the new economy offers freedom that the old, more paternalistic regime could not. The steady stream of success stories that poured out of Silicon Valley and Alley were those of people who think outside the box, who participate in what author Daniel Pink calls the "free agent nation," who revel in being a self-governing unit, who seem to have little need for being taken care of.

This new model, however, simply does not speak to the emotional needs of many Americans. For those who turn to the workplace for commitment, stability, and care, the new economy is filled with land mines of confusion and betrayal. As many people approach their jobs with selfobject longing, seeking recognition and validation that is unavailable in other arenas of their lives, corporations increasingly want flexibility and intense, but only short-lived, loyalty. The unqualified acceptance of change is paramount.

Robert Reich, former secretary of labor, captures this new regime well when he points out: "Increasingly in the new economy, the only way up is to promote yourself . . . In the new economy, you get ahead not by being well liked but by being well marketed." What he means by well marketed is that no matter where you are in the job hierarchy, you treat yourself as a business. As management guru Tom Peters tells the normative American employee: "Starting today you are a brand. You're every bit as much a brand as Nike, Coke, Pepsi, or the Body Shop." If you are to succeed, your "most important job is to be head marketer for the brand called You." Peters' latest book, *The Brand You 50: Or: Fifty Ways to Transform Yourself from an "Employee" into a Brand That Shouts Distinction, Commitment, and Passion!,* is a blatant call to transform the self into an instrumental object that is constituted and directed by the market. It fundamentally eschews a self that longs for true recognition and acceptance. Instead, it places a premium on those of us who can shift our needs and personae to accommodate the twists and turns of today's economy. It assumes that we all have the capacity to commit completely and passionately to today's job and leave it tomorrow without looking back. It is the Gestalt Prayer repackaged for the new economy.

What is bedrock here is change. "Today," Robert Reich announces in *Fast Company* magazine's issue entitled "*Your* Job Is Change," "Change has changed—the speed, the pace, the type, the purpose. The balance has shifted. . . . Companies that can't change in this new environment can't play in this new economy." What is needed are "change insurgents," people who accept, facilitate, and promote *constant* change within an organization. "The change insurgent has to keep altering the organization's fundamental form, focusing on its capacity to change constantly." "Change today means that companies need shit disturbers, not ass kissers." The worst quality an employee can evince is a tendency to resist change. In fact, Reich insists, it is crucial for companies to detect change resisters in their midst, and provides a list of statements an employee might make that would indicate that he or she is resistant to change. Examples are: "Let's go back to the basics." "It worked before." "The numbers don't work." "That seems risky." If an employee makes one of these incriminating statements, he or she should be coaxed along to new consciousness, to recognizing that change is good, change is all there is. Reich, however, makes the bottom line perfectly clear: "The game is changing, and they [change resisters] can either play within the new rules or play somewhere else."

In the new economy, valuing history, loyalty, time for reflection, thoughtfulness, and a genuine respect for others' opinions that are outside the change-insurgent norm, is not only outmoded but denigrated. It signals that one is part of the old economic order. In many ways, I think Lionel was seen as outmoded. At forty-five, he had been with VPA for twenty-seven years. He felt extremely proud of that longevity, and thought that his ability to talk about company history, how things were done in the past, would earn him respect. He reports, however, that each time he did make such a comment, especially to his new, thirty-year-old supervisor, he was greeted with responses such as "That was then, this is now," or, "Thanks for letting us know, Lionel." Then the conversation would move on. Lionel could never understand why his accumulated knowledge, his insights into company culture and history, weren't valued. Undoubtedly, the implicit contract Lionel thought he had signed when he first joined VPA in 1973—that he and the company would grow old together, that he would be taken care of if he performed well, that his stature in the company would increase with his longevity—had changed. Rather than being a respected, senior member of the organization, he was an anachronism, an embarrassment.

How much Lionel must have been perceived as a flagrant change resister was revealed in a meeting he told me about, in which his team was discussing eliminating offices and cubicles in order to streamline work flow. Apparently Lionel announced that such an idea "would never work around here. Everyone here really loves their own space and wants to move up to a better one." This invocation of tradition, the unwillingness to accept change, probably branded him as a hopeless deadweight, but Lionel could never quite get over the absurdity of the suggestion of eliminating offices. It struck him as an incomprehensible idea, signaling to him that "Maybe things are going in a way that I really can't fit in anymore."

It strikes me that Lionel's incomprehension, his sense that the workplace was changing in a fundamental way that he couldn't fathom, was important. I certainly thought the same thing after getting to know Jim, and hearing about how the organization of his office space affected him emotionally.

The advertising agency that Jim worked for was located in a converted warehouse in San Francisco. It had no interior walls. Everybody, from the president to the receptionist, sat at desks in an open area. As it turns out, this organization of work space is part of a new trend. According to Malcolm Gladwell:

> In the eighties and early nineties, the fashion in corporate America was to follow what designers called "universal planning"—rows of identical cubicles. . . . Today, universal planning has fallen out of favor. . . . If you visit the technology companies of Silicon Valley, or the media companies of Manhattan, or any of the firms that self-consciously identify themselves with the New Economy, you'll find that secluded private offices have been replaced by busy public spaces, open-plan areas without walls, executives next to the newest hires.

For many people, this change represents a democratic shift, a turn away from hierarchy and privilege in the way in which corporations are organized. And in many ways, this seems true. But it is not without its costs from an emotional or psychological point of view. Without walls, every move, affect, or behavior can be witnessed by others—both one's supervisors and supervisees. To exist in such a public setting for eight, ten, twelve hours a day requires a remarkable degree of self-monitoring and emotional control. This is particularly true when something upsetting occurs at work. Jim told me early on in our sessions:

> I never liked that setup. It's really hard when I'm tired, when my defenses are down, when I just want to put my head down on my desk and veg out. But no, that's definitely not okay. . . . There's nowhere to go to let off steam. . . . There are only two bathrooms and you can't really go in there too much because people see that, too.

When Jim's boss, the firm's president, informed him that a client was unhappy about an advertising campaign Jim had managed, he talked to Jim at his, the president's, desk in the center of the cavernous office. The shame and humiliation Jim experienced in light of the president's rebuke was exacerbated by the setting in which the conversation occurred.

> It just felt like a public lynching. He wasn't talking loud, but I know people could tell what was going on. I mean, you work in an environment for that long and people get awfully good at reading each other without hearing exactly what you're saying. . . . It used to be after something like that you'd walk in the office and close the door, maybe cry or scream or whatever. But now I have to walk back to my desk like some fucking Gary Cooper character and pretend that everything's okay, you know, I'm a man, I can take it, when inside I want to curl up in a ball and die.

It was this "public lynching" that sent Jim into a deep depression and a reassessment of his life. But it was also the daily experience of self-monitoring, of feeling that he was working in a panopticon, that wore away at Jim's psychological reserves. "Everyday I had to gear up to go in there because I felt I always had to be on; everyone could see. . . . It got harder to figure out what was me, what was I really feeling, and what was an act."

Jim's predicament raises larger social questions as employers do away with walls and workplace surveillance increases. "According to a 1999 survey by the American Management Association, two-thirds of employers record employee voice mail, e-mail, or phone calls, review computer files, or videotape workers, and such surveillance is becoming more common. Rights of free speech and privacy that are essential to public deliberation and private solidarity are, to put it mildly, insecure in the workplace." What is also insecure is people's ability to have privacy, feelings, and experience outside the gaze of others— others who can control time, salary, and status and who can fire—despite how democratically the desks might be arranged.

Thus, as many of us turn to our workplaces with selfobject yearnings, attempting to find the attention, care, and recognition that family and community are ceasing to provide, the emotional requirements for survival in the new economic order may be too great, at odds with many people's needs. We are asked to work intensely, passionately, and with commitment, but only in the short term. We are not supposed to worry about what our supervisor or coworkers really think of us, but only how well we can market ourselves to them to enhance our future employability. We must cast aside anxiety about uncertain futures and think only of the benefits of risk taking and change insurgency. We cannot hold onto our connections or allegiance to the past, lest we be seen as a drag on our employers. We must be flexible, upbeat, and self-confident, and be so increasingly in the full view of others, but these others are not those who pro vide the time and attention necessary for a sense of an unfolding interior to emerge. Increasingly we are to view our fellow employees only as a transitory audience in front of whom we market the brand called *Us*.

"Divorce" in an Empty Arena

When the personality is for sale, all relationships turn into business deals.

—Robert Reich

The psychological expectations emanating from the new economy appear to be affecting different industries at different rates. Clearly, those organizations involved in high tech, biotech, and the mass media have led the change-insurgency movement. But I would argue that this relatively new orientation to work has seeped into our more general cultural assumptions regarding employment in America, and that it affects all of us, regardless of where we are employed.

Most of my patients encounter these assumptions after they have experienced a work failure—a layoff or betrayal at their job. In trying to cope with this, they find themselves not only facing their employers' disregard, but also encountering a similar indifference by family, friends, and professionals to whom they turn for help. Such indifference is echoed throughout our society.

After each of my patients' employer or supervisor, such as Grace's Tanya, or Marion's Bill, turned against him or her, each felt traumatized by what he or she experienced as a profound betrayal. The trauma was exacerbated by the fact that no one in their respective companies acknowledged what had happened, "no one cared." The highly valued organization—Marion's Phaeton, Lionel's VPA, Sarah's PeoplePoint—suddenly became an indifferent institution, whereas it had previously been a family or welcoming team of like-minded people. Each of these employees found him or herself caught up in a contradiction that seemed incomprehensible. "What I had to say was supposed to count." "This place was like a home to me." "I thought they cared." But, alas, they didn't. Suddenly, the idealized selfobject in the form of a direct supervisor, or the institution itself, no longer appeared to care. The self-sustaining functions that the workplace supplied abruptly ended. The needed glue holding parts of the self together began to dissolve, and the solidity of life seemed to be melting into air.

Each employee felt a stunning sense of loneliness and isolation. In some cases, such as with Grace, Jim, and Michelle, they literally couldn't imagine whom they might call to talk about their work problems. For others, such as Brenda, Luba, and, to a lesser degree, Sarah and Marion, there were family and/or friends in their lives. In each of these cases, however, my patients report that they were greeted with a remarkable lack of empathy. No one could understand why they were as upset as they were. So the trauma of betrayal was amplified by the fact that they felt utterly alone with their experience.

What is striking is how much this incredulity and indifference is echoed by medical doctors and psychotherapists, who often view their patients' work lives as of secondary importance in relation to what is *really* significant, that is, family and personal relationships. Primary-care physicians and therapists often instruct patients to return to work as soon as possible or to simply find new jobs, without beginning to acknowledge the emotional investment that has been made in a particular job, a particular supervisor, or corporation. While no one would tell a patient to simply go find a new wife as he is going through a divorce, it is all too common for health professionals to see jobs and workplaces as interchangeable.

In our second session, Jim told me that he first confided to his internist that he thought he was depressed because of some problems at work, and was surprised by his doctor's response. "He just immediately said I shouldn't let work get me down, that there were a million opportunities out there for a young man like me, and maybe I needed a vacation. He then proceeded to tell me about the safari he had just gone on."

Marion went to her primary-care doctor for multiple visits during the time that her relationship with her boss, Bill, was declining. When Marion would tell her about the stress she was experiencing at work, her physician told her, "All jobs are stressful these days; you've just got to live with it." After Bill shouted at her, and Marion felt as though her life were over, she went to see this same doctor, who recognized that her patient was clinically depressed. She referred Marion to a psychiatrist who apparently didn't get it:

"I mean, this guy was nice and everything, but he kept saying that he couldn't believe I could be this upset about a job, that I must be depressed because I was single or because my kids were getting older, going to leave home and all. I thought, 'Boy, I really must be a nut.'"

Sarah also went to see another therapist before meeting with me. In this case, her human-resources department referred her to an outplacement counselor:

"She was no help at all. She was as ga-ga about PeoplePoint as me and thought how angry I was was just really crazy. After I saw her two times I felt much worse because she made me feel that *I* was the problem, that there was something wrong with *me*."

These therapists' insensitivity to their patients' sense of emotional devastation is undoubtedly fueled by clinical theories that remain silent about our relationship to the workplace. In this respect, the world of psychotherapy has changed little from the early part of the twentieth century when Freud wrote:

> As a path to happiness, work is not highly prized by men. They do not strive after it as they do after other possibilities of satisfaction. The great majority of people only work under the stress of necessity, and this natural aversion to work raises most difficult social problems.

When work appears in clinical case studies, it serves as a backdrop to the "real" stage on which people experience the vicissitudes of their emotional lives, that is, the family and romantic relationships. The fact that most of us spend the majority of our waking hours at work, and invest huge parts of our emotional resources there, is not reflected in clinical thinking. As one of the very few clinicians writing about work, Steven Axelrod notes that psychotherapists "are too quick to shift the focus from the content of work life to early development or the transference, thereby subtly neglecting the full richness of our patients' work lives." Author Vince Bielski adds, "Obliviousness to work issues isn't surprising considering that questions of work-identity often dominate therapists' own lives in the age of managed care. Therapists don't see the problem in others because they don't see it in themselves."

When patients' feelings about what happens to them on the job are dismissed by doctors or therapists, their belief that there is something profoundly wrong with them—"boy, I must really be a nut"—is amplified. It signals to them that no one who is healthy, mature, or reasonable could be affected by work as they are. It heightens their sense of isolation, the feeling that they should keep their feelings of emptiness and loss to themselves. To reveal what they truly feel opens them up to being shamed and humiliated. If a professional authority figure finds your emotions and responses incomprehensible, then surely you are overreacting, immature, or mentally ill. If "all jobs these days are stressful," or if "there are a million jobs out there" that are interchangeable, then you are overreacting; *you* are the problem. When Jim, Marion, and Sarah met with indifference by the professionals to whom they turned, they felt worse.

This sense of personal responsibility and personal failure does not emanate merely from professionals' offices; it resounds throughout our society. We simply have no vocabulary with which to talk about feelings of betrayal, loss, and torment in the workplace. We are a society that values overwork, one that equates it with success, mental health, and personal fulfillment. However, when it ends, when we feel we have to leave or are forced to leave our jobs, suddenly work is nothing; it carries no emotional weight. Being angry, disgruntled, or bitter for a while is okay, but feeling bereft, empty, and/or emotionally devastated has no place. And certainly having such feelings for weeks or months is a sign of true irrationality and instability. Our task in the twenty-first century is to invest everything we have in our jobs, to make work personal, then walk away without looking back if something goes wrong. If we cannot manage this emotionally, we have only ourselves to blame. It is our inadequacy.

Richard Sennett writes:

> Today, late Victorian values of personal responsibility are as strong as a century ago, but their institutional context has changed. The iron cage has been dismantled, so that individuals struggle for security and coherence in a seemingly empty arena. The destruction of institutional supports at work, as in the welfare state, leaves individuals only their sense of responsibility; the Victorian ethos now often charts a negative trajectory of defeated will, of having failed to make one's life cohere through one's work. . . . This sense of personal responsibility deflects workers' anger away from economic institutions to themselves.

Because there are so few institutional anchors, so little that feels stable and secure outside work, a failure in one's job can feel terrifying. And because our society provides no way of understanding that failure other than through the language of individual responsibility, our sense of being utterly alone, utterly to blame, can be all we have.

In comparison, when an intimate relationship fails or when we go through a divorce, we are surrounded by resources, systems of meaning, and a highly developed vocabulary to describe our experience. Everyone we turn to is sympathetic. Professionals remind us that, on average, it takes two years to recover from a divorce. Self-help books, magazines, talk shows, and weekend workshops offer endless ways of coping with our sense of loss, self-blame, and identity crisis. We can come to understand what we are experiencing through a lexi-con that says that men are from Mars and women from Venus, or that we are codependent, or that we are among the unfortu-nates who love too much. We can attend twelve-step meetings offered throughout our communities for CODAs (codepen-dents anonymous) or for sex-and-love addicts. We can follow prescribed steps to cope with our bereavement and, all along, have our sense of displacement acknowledged and understood by those around us. We may feel we have failed, but it is a fail-ure that is socially and culturally comprehensible. With the comforting knowledge that fifty percent of marriages end in divorce, we know we are not alone.

This context of meaning does not exist when it comes to a workplace divorce. Because of this, my patients feel there is no end to their shame and sense of failure. They often speak in the language of an abyss, an endless void that opens up before them in their exile from the workplace. Without words to describe their experience, without others to fully understand, without families and communities to feed back to them a sense of iden-tity and place, they express themselves through physical symp-toms or repeated laments of "I thought they cared"; "I knew that it was over"; "I have no place to go." They are emotional nomads, because their experience cannot find a home, a socially sanctioned context for making their feelings understandable to them.

Thus, the emotional landscape of work in the twenty-first century offers us an array of emotional challenges rarely ac-knowledged or appreciated. At a time when so many of us are turning to the workplace for the satisfaction of unmet selfob-ject needs, we are being asked to work continually, intensely, and passionately but only in the short term. As the social fabric around us frays, and our connections to others feel increasingly fragmented and ephemeral, we are asked to be change insurgents who not only accept continuous change in the workplace, but value it as a way of life. We are to eschew safety and security and, instead, welcome endless flexibility and risk. If we experience a failure at work, we are to move on, remembering that the marketing of the self is all we can rely on.

Given these formidable challenges, what continues to make the workplace such an inviting place for so many of us? How do we get seduced into marriage and remarriage to our jobs? After what she had experienced at the import–export business and our months of therapy together, why did Michelle allow herself to marry yet another job? To answer these questions, we cannot look only at the emotional needs people bring to the workplace. We must also discover what is being offered by corporations today that makes them so enticing. We must peer into the twenty-first-century workplace, one that is increasingly designed not merely for work but for living one's life. For it is in the intersection of people's unfilled needs and corporate interests that the sacrament of marriage is enacted.

CHAPTER FOUR

On the Difference Between Eggs and Bacon

The difference between the old and new economies is like eggs and bacon. The old is like the chicken—merely involved. The new is like the pig—totally committed.
—SILICON VALLEY ADAGE

THE AMERICAN WORKPLACE has undergone a significant transformation. Throughout the 1990s, corporations subscribed to beliefs about how to manage employees that made workplaces more emotionally compelling. As *Fortune* magazine declared in 2000: the "new workplace is not just a place to work. It's a place to live." In order to attract and retain employees, corporate America caught on to people's unmet emotional needs better than any other segment of society—including organized religion, political parties, trade unions, or volunteer organizations. The corporate workplace offered replacement communities and families. It spoke to people's desire to identify with something larger than themselves that was powerful and respected, or, conversely, innovative and scrappy (the Apple paradigm). It provided a growing number of amenities, a greater appearance of equality and democracy in its organization, and an increasing emphasis on company *culture*.

It is now a fundamental business management assumption

that what distinguishes the leading companies is their robust cultures:

> A robust culture in a cohesive enterprise is committed to a deep and abiding shared purpose. Its robustness is highly dependent on a unifying cultural tapestry woven over time as people cooperate and learn together. It is woven from the interplay of a set of interlocking cultural elements: History yields values. Values create focus and shape behavior. Heroic figures exemplify core values and beliefs. Ritual and ceremony dramatize values and summon the collective spirit. Stories broadcast heroic exploits, reinforce core values, and provide delightful material for company events.

The ideal company envelops its employees in shared values and purpose, provides identity within the corporate embrace, and idealizes the heroic CEO or company founder through workplace rituals.

As the authors of *Fortune's* annual report on the "100 Best Companies to Work For," Robert Levering and Milton Moskowitz, point out: "A century ago the most valuable United States corporation was U.S. Steel, whose primary assets were smokestack factories. Today's most valuable corporation is Microsoft, whose most valuable assets go home every night."

In order to retain and enhance the performance of these most valuable assets, corporations cater not only to their employees' need for compensation but to their emotional longings as well. In their book *The New Corporate Cultures,* Terrence Deal and Allan Kennedy assert that the role culture plays in performance seems obvious . . . When people are vested in their work, they work harder, show up on time, stay late when needed, and take pride in the company's products or services. They are loyal, committed, and interested in the collective welfare as well as their individual careers. They speak up when things need to be changed rather than signing off or shipping out. Not only hands *but their heads and hearts* are engaged in the enterprise's mission [emphasis added].

Creating an emotionally evocative company culture in order to produce hard-working, loyal employees is the commonly invoked management philosophy touted by many of today's "heroic figures." Starbucks CEO Howard Schultz claims that if "people relate to the company they work for, if they form an emotional tie to it and buy into its dream, they will pour their hearts into making it better." Herb Kelleher, CEO of Southwest Airlines, states that "Culture is one of the most precious things a company has, so you must work harder on it than anything else." In order to facilitate this belief, Kelleher publicly tells his employees that he loves them and asserts that Southwest is "the airline that love built."

Within these corporate cultures of "emotional ties" and "love," organizational hierarchies are flattened. There are fewer middle managers, more accessibility to vice presidents and CEOs, less formality, greater emphasis on teamwork, and transparency. Company presidents often work out of cubicles and wear the same t-shirts and jeans as their administrative assistants. They may all participate in company beer bashes and play together in company athletic leagues. Employees tend to work on teams in which everyone's input is elicited in order to execute short-time projects. And, increasingly, corporate decisions and finances are available to all employees via the company intranet, allowing information that was once confidential to be transparently revealed to all.

In the most advanced segments of this new corporate environment, employees in the 1990s encountered amenities never dreamed about a decade prior. In *Fortune* magazine's "100 Best Companies to Work For," it was common to find not only corporate child care, free food, and weekly parties, but take-home meals, school tuition, full-service gyms, concierge services, support groups, company rock bands, paid time off for volunteer work, massage, sabbaticals, in-house stores, and all-company trips to tropical islands.

Gymboree, a retailer of children's clothing, offered recess, with games of hopscotch and four-square, to its employees at its headquarters in Silicon Valley. Software maker SAS Institute in Cary, North Carolina, had an on-site health center with physicians and dentists. At Rodale, a publisher of health and fitness materials, employees gardened on company plots. JM Family Enterprises, a Toyota distributor in Florida, provided its workers with free haircuts and manicures. BMC Software in Houston had a car wash. And Sun Microsystems in Palo Alto, California, offered SunSpots—rooms for rest or meditation, and SunRooms, for table tennis, pinball, or trash-can basketball.

At Michelle's new workplace, a corporate culture that stressed "work as fun," amenities, and teamwork was simply too alluring for a twenty-six-year-old with tremendous dependency needs. Watching her supervisor, Shelby, work hard and play hard in this culture seduced Michelle into an almost cultlike devotion. She wanted to both be accepted by Shelby and be Shelby. Her new employer offered status in the outside world and an ongoing partylike atmosphere at work. She reveled in the three-story slide, Friday beer busts and free food. She felt catered to and privileged by the dry cleaning and concierge services provided. Her team accepted her, loved her baked goods and offered a ready-made group of friends who seemed more attentive than her family of origin. With all of this, Michelle became a "pig—totally committed."

To summarize the ways in which work in the new economy differed from the model that prevailed throughout much of the twentieth century, *Business 2.0,* a magazine that chronicles the current world of work, provides a concise synopsis:

THE OLD WAY	THE NEW WAY
Security	Opportunity
Detachment	Total Commitment
Hierarchy	We're All Equal
Work and Fun Don't Mix	Pamper Me
It's Just a Job	It's So Much More

For many Americans, this new way was a form of liberation, challenge, and excitement. The secure, self-directed individual could realize his or her potential, exercise creativity, and truly have fun at work. Business magazines such as *Fast Company, Red Herring,* and *Business 2.0* routinely heralded the numerous success stories of the new economy—people who utilized the new work environment to achieve and genuinely thrive. However, what never appeared in any of these publications were the stories of the women and men who lost themselves in the new way. These are the employees who thoroughly immerse themselves in company culture, values, and purpose.

They believe wholeheartedly in the new way. They subscribe to *total commitment,* assume that *we're all equal,* and decisively reject the idea that *it's just a job.* They so completely give themselves to the new way that their sense of who they are becomes a function of work.

Because of its emphasis on total commitment, on being a substitute family, I believe the new-way workplace more easily speaks to people's unmet emotional needs than the old way did. If work is just a job based on emotional detachment, rigid hierarchy, and the absence of fun, it is more difficult to elicit feelings of belonging, being recognized and valued, and part of something that invokes "heroism," "collective spirit," "collective welfare," "dreams," and "mission." In light of the decline of family, community, and civic life, what the workplace of the new economy offers can be a lifeline, an emotional haven in an otherwise insecure and anomic world.

WORK AS FAMILY

Teri joined my group-therapy program at the beginning of 2000. She is thirty-four, significantly overweight, sports a nose ring, and has a flower tattooed on her forearm. She is gregarious and affable. Teri is the only child of a teenage mother. She grew up in the Central Valley of California and completed high school. Because her mother was "so young and wild," Teri spent much of her childhood being shuffled around to different extended family members' homes. She claims that all of these relatives were warm and accepting of her but that she frequently felt out of place and like an intruder. Teri spent little time in school focusing on course work or grades, but devoted her energies to her many friends, both girls and boys. She was often the class cut-up and was known as a kid who liked to have a good time.

After high school, Teri found a job working in a family child-care center located in the home of a friend of her aunt's. She enjoyed the work immensely, suddenly discovering that she had a gift for caring for small children. For a number of years, she spent eight to ten hours a day working at the child-care center, then partied in the evenings with her friends. This life suited her well, until a number of her friends got married and her credit-card debt began to overwhelm her. Teri, who remained single, spent more evenings alone and more time worrying about money. She earned $8.50 per hour, which couldn't cover her expenses, no matter how much she tried to economize. With great difficulty, Teri admitted to herself that it was time to move on, to find more remunerative work and a wider social circle. She began searching for a new job and, after many months of interviewing, was hired by a new corporate child-care center near San Jose.

Sinclair Systems, Inc. had just constructed a fully equipped, state-of-the-art child care center that could accommodate 35 children at a time for its employees. Teri was hired at $13.50 per hour, a dramatic increase in her earnings, and was suddenly introduced to a corporate world she hadn't known existed. She had a full week of orientation to both Sinclair Systems in general, and the Care Center at Sinclair Systems, Inc., itself, which everyone called "Cassie" (for CCASS,I). Teri's new employer fully subscribed to the new way, and touted Cassie as an example of how much the company cared about and for its employees.

Margaret, the newly hired Cassie director, had been a special-needs administrator at a nearby unified school district before coming to Sinclair. Her new corporate position apparently filled her with an immense amount of pride, enthusiasm, and energy for Cassie's possibilities. In her orientation with her new staff, Margaret seemed to expect a great deal of dedication, commitment, and time from her employees. Teri reports that Margaret tried to inspire them to believe that they weren't just taking a job but were part of a new era of putting the needs of children first.

Teri found herself not only agreeing with Margaret's message, but wanting nothing more than to make Cassie a complete success. When Margaret asked who would like to volunteer to chair various committees having to do with training, special events, parents' nights, and employee potlucks, Teri eagerly put herself forward. She said, "Somehow this whole thing about putting children first really got to me. I just wanted to be part of it. I wanted it to work."

Teri became Margaret's first lieutenant, and was intimately aware of how her supervisor envisioned the care center operating. Margaret believed the staff should act as a substitute family for its charges and, in turn, become a family to each other. Margaret so frequently invoked images of family life to her staff that Teri became increasingly aware of the role—or lack thereof—of her own family in her life. In order to take the job at Cassie, Teri had had to move to be closer to work, and had little contact with her relatives. Because most of her friends had married and were having children of their own, Teri talked to them less and saw them infrequently. For the first time in her life, she acknowledged that she felt lonely, and consciously turned to work to fill the emotional emptiness she experienced.

From the day she started group therapy, Teri spoke clearly and insightfully about her emotional involvement in her job.

She described moving into a two-bedroom apartment with another woman with whom she had little in common, and feeling lonely and disconnected living in the San Jose area in order to work at Cassie. With little else to occupy her, she increasingly devoted all of her energies to making the care center a substitute family for the children, and for herself. Given that this was her supervisor's intent, Teri and Margaret worked in tandem to make Cassie as homelike as possible, and to involve the staff in their workplace family. Margaret specifically scheduled staff meetings between five and seven in the evening as potluck dinners to enable her employees to be able to break bread together. When some of the other child-care workers objected—some were single mothers who needed to be home with their children—Teri vociferously defended Margaret's decision, and thus began to alienate herself from her coworkers. This alienation only intensified when Teri agreed with Margaret that attendance at the Sinclair annual holiday party should be required. Many of Cassie's employees felt they didn't fit in with the high-tech, corporate culture of Sinclair. They resented the haughty attitudes and high pay of the other employees, and felt a world apart tucked away in the care center, which was in a separate building across the highway from headquarters. Many said they wouldn't feel comfortable at the party, but Margaret and Teri saw this as a betrayal of the family offered by Sinclair, and were personally affronted.

As her coworkers increasingly began to complain about their work; about the corporate culture at Sinclair, which they found disingenuous; and about Margaret's overly zealous leadership, Teri found herself more defensive of the company and more a supporter of the idea that Cassie should be a family. Teri remarks that "if you had asked me then I would have said 'this is the best job in the world.' I loved the kids and I loved Margaret and, honestly, I loved Sinclair."

As the months passed, Teri describes feeling increasingly anxious and depressed when she was away from her job. Weekends began to terrify her, because she had nothing to do, no one to call. She was losing contact with her friends and family at home, and couldn't find a way to connect with people in San Jose. She could not imagine where she might meet like-minded peers. Thus, she threw herself into planning Cassie social events with a zeal that was incomprehensible to her coworkers. Teri states that even Margaret began to grow weary of her boundless enthusiasm about how to improve relations with parents, how to enrich the time for children at the center, how to bring together the increasingly alienated staff.

In November 1999, Margaret and Teri came up with the idea of keeping the child-care center open on New Year's Eve as a gift to Sinclair employees. When Margaret approached Sinclair management with their proposal, she was lavishly praised and given the go-ahead. Shortly thereafter, Teri received a letter from the Director of Human Resources praising her for her commitment to Cassie and the "entire Sinclair Systems family," and giving her a $300 gift certificate from a local department store "to make this holiday season a memorable one." Teri was joyful about this recognition.

Margaret and Teri began planning how they would spend their New Year's Eve: They would buy party favors for the parents who dropped off their children; they would have a special Y2K party for their charges; they would wear dresses; and they would carefully choose which of the staff would participate with them in this event. Thus, Teri was shocked at her coworkers' reactions when Margaret brought up the plan at a staff meeting. "I actually thought that people would want to do this. It sounded so fun. But when they heard they weren't getting paid for it, nobody wanted it. They acted as though we were crazy."

It was after that meeting that Teri began to reflect on her life. "I got home and thought, for the first time, 'I'm pathetic.' Instead of resenting everybody at work for not caring, I started thinking 'maybe it's me; maybe the problem is me, not them.'" Her reaction to these thoughts was to become quite depressed. She started sleeping and eating more. However, it was not until the much anticipated New Year's Eve arrived that the full force of her depression hit. "We were completely full. In fact, there was a waiting list. All the parents were so happy. At the beginning of the night, I felt really good. But, as it got closer to midnight and most of the kids were asleep, I started to sink."

For the next week, Teri could barely get out of bed. She states that she was simply overwhelmed with the recognition that she didn't have a life, and was trying to make Cassie her family. A few weeks later, she joined one of my psychotherapy groups.

From her first day in group, Teri has been an invaluable asset, because she clearly articulates what so many of the other women are only able to feel. She looked to her workplace as a substitute family, and she did this with the support and encouragement of her immediate supervisor and the corporation for which she worked. Teri's emotional commitment, loyalty, and long hours, the way in which she gave not only her "hands," but her "head and heart" to her job, qualifies her as an ideal employee in the new economic order. However, it ultimately left Teri feeling alone and depressed.

As real family life declines, the new economy has "made

business synonymous with life. . . . Coworkers are now family; friends are colleagues, and community is a staff meeting," according to Jonathan Keats in his article "It's the End of Work as We Know It."

At the very least, management that stresses the creation of corporate cultures lends itself to employees viewing workplaces as fictive families. At most, corporations intentionally use the words and imagery of family to solidify company cultures and inspire loyalty and commitment in an attempt to boost productivity. Wal-Mart explicitly uses invocations of family to promote corporate solidarity and oppose unionization. During a recent attempt to unionize workers at a Wal-Mart store in Wisconsin, the store's new comanager showed antiunion videos to employees, who are known as associates, and she cried as she begged the workers not to "invite a third party into the Wal-Mart family." After staff meetings focused on the "Wal-Mart cheer" ("Give me a W. Give me an A . . ."), the associates, that is, workers, rejected the union's bid.

At the New York City headquarters of Steelcase, Inc., one of the world's leading designers and manufacturers of office furniture, the company installed a six-by-four-foot glass case filled with 1,500 ants as a demonstration of how "families live and work together." According to Steelcase's Dave Lathrop, this display positively demonstrated how "work and non-work are blending . . . Ants live to work and work to live." At the software company PeopleSoft, Tina Cox, manager of employee communications, states flatly: "We are a family." The founder and former CEO of the company, David A. Duffield, routinely sent out all of his e-mail under his initials, DAD. And, when queried about work–family balance, the chief of Human Relations at Houston's BMC Software, Roy Wilson, said that, due to the company's many amenities, BMC "gives you a balanced life without having to leave."

My patients report ways in which allusions to family have been commonplace at their jobs. Sarah's employer routinely played "We Are Family" by Sister Sledge at company parties and picnics. VPA, Lionel's corporation, published a monthly employee newsletter with a column titled "Happenings in the VPA Family." When Marion was hired at Phaeton, Bill welcomed her "into our family."

Such explicit references, however, are not necessary for employees to feel that work is family and home. According to sociologist Helen Mederer, recognizing that work is "becoming home for many people, companies are taking the best aspects of home and incorporating them into work." "Pick just about any aspect of private life, and it's being subsumed into the workplace," notes Jerry Useem of *Fortune* magazine:

> Start with domestic chores: 46 of the 100 Best Companies offer take-home meals to liberate people from having to cook dinner. Twenty-six of the 100 offer personal concierge services, allowing employees to outsource the time consuming details of buying flowers and birthday presents, planning bar mitzvahs, or, in the case of one Chicago suitor, organizing an engagement dinner. . . . LesConcierges in San Francisco estimates that each dollar spent to provide its services yields $1.75 in gained employee productivity.

As increasing numbers of mothers with newborns return quickly to their jobs, employers are offering help with breast feeding. Hundreds of corporations, including "Aetna, Eastman Kodak, Cigna, and Home Depot, now offer 'lactation support rooms' . . . [and] 'lactation consultants' . . . Aetna . . . estimates that it saves $1,435 and three days of sick leave per breast-fed baby."

Babies and dogs are entering workplaces. According to Pam Belluck, reporter for the *New York Times,* "a growing number of employers are allowing parents to bring their babies to work, not to an on-site day care center, but directly to their desks, where they care for their children while doing their jobs. . . . [E]mployers have found that allowing babies to accompany parents to work keeps companies from losing valuable employees and sometimes brings mothers back from maternity leave sooner. It is a fringe benefit that employers say costs almost nothing." Dogs are also increasingly welcomed. Given that "many offices these days are as formal as backyard barbecues," according to *Times* reporter Lisa Foderaro, "employees say they bring their dogs to work simply because they hate to leave them home alone." And, as we saw in chapter 2, given that most homes are emptied of people during the day, it makes sense that the workplace would be absorbing those non-human creatures left behind.

Far more significant than these sorts of developments are the ways in which many Americans' personal identities are increasingly constructed through their jobs. As one employee interviewed by sociologist Arlie Hochschild for her book *The Time Bind* succinctly puts it: "In America, we don't have family coats of arms anymore, but we have the company logo."

It is this sentiment that I find over and over again among my patients. In many of my group-therapy sessions, I have had the experience of looking around the room at the assembled women who feel exiled from the world of work, the jobs they loved, and have noted the number sporting T-shirts, caps, and sweatshirts with their former employer's logo. As my patients speak of their grief over their separation from their work-places—the source of identity for so many of them—I can't help but think that wearing that shirt or cap remains a means of staying connected to their fictive families, of proclaiming to the world and to themselves that they are still part of the People-Point, or Phaeton, or Sinclair lineage. Logos provide a form of instant recognition, an immediate way of being known in the world that in prior ages the surname Cohen, McCoy, or Windsor might have afforded. Employees voicelessly signal that they are institutionally anchored in a world that is anonymous, opaque, and fragmented. And, when the corporation is widely known or highly respected, they can bask in the reflected glory of their employer. I assume this is the motivation for the workers at Nike who have the company's logo, the swoosh, tattooed on their ankles.

With the increasing emphasis on corporate branding, and the instant, nonverbal recognition that it evokes in consumers, companies value their employees displaying the corporate logo everywhere they go. This not only builds workers' embrace of the all-important company culture, but provides a free form of advertising. Company stores have been a feature of the new economy workplace. When workers are feeling lost, lonely, unanchored in an environment of increasingly small and frag-mented families, these stores can help shape a sense of belong-ing and identity.

Sarah is an extreme example of this. She describes literally trying to cover her house and her children in the PeoplePoint logo. Because her employer was so large, and such a force in the economy of the late 1990s, it offered more than the typical t-shirt, coffee mug, and pen. Its company store sold PeoplePoint children's clothes, book bags, backpacks, key rings, and dishes. Sarah bought them all. She can now laugh at this behavior:

"Sometimes I would go out in the morning with the kids, taking them to day care, and we'd all be PeoplePoint people. I mean I had them *covered* with junk from there. And I'd be so proud, you know, 'I work at PeoplePoint, I'm really great . . .' Now I think people must have thought 'she's crazy.'"

Many probably did think Sarah and her sons were excessive. Most likely, however, no one thought it strange in general to wear the name of one's employer on one's back or chest or head. Most of us do not permanently tattoo our employer's name on our bodies but, each day that we don our company's baseball cap or sweatshirt, we brand ourselves not unlike ranch animals, proclaiming to the world to whom we belong.

This kind of branding also occurs when employees proudly proclaim that they are Sofites or Microserfs, because they work at Microsoft; Scitorians because they work at Scitor; Micro-strategists, because they work at MicroStrategy, or Screamers, because they work at Screaming Media.

Throughout history people have marked time by holidays and community celebrations. Although Americans enjoy far fewer holidays than people in preindustrial societies, we still measure the passage of time by its punctuation with holidays such as Thanksgiving, Christmas, and Easter. Traditionally, many of these days have been ones that bring together family, allowing us to reaffirm our identities and sense of belonging. Among the patients I see, however, the most important holidays generally have been those that have been invented by the companies for which they work. It is the company's summer picnic or holiday party or annual convention that becomes the marker of time. In my groups, members have spoken about how "I couldn't go to the [company holiday] party looking like this, so I figured I had two months to lose fifteen pounds." "I guess I kind of lived for those parties." "My whole year focused around preparing for and recovering from the convention in June." Brenda, whose failure to be present at the annual Christmas party initiated her workplace downfall, describes what these events meant to her:

> I had never been to anything like them. They were fantastic. They really went all out with the food and an open bar. . . . I loved thinking about what I was going to wear. . . . The best part was that I got to see all the clients that we had worked with and sometimes people who used to work at the firm but had moved on. It was like a reunion, and I felt a part of this really big family, sort of this glamorous family that was rich and could entertain and be very generous to everyone.

After her first two years with the law firm, Brenda was asked to coordinate these parties. She describes how the anticipation of this event structured her entire year: "I would think, okay, it's March, and in only seven more months I'll have to go to the printer with the invitations and then I'll have to meet with the caterer." These responsibilities were not part of her job description, nor was she remunerated for all her planning and work. These issues miss the point, however. The firm's Christmas party gave her life a certain direction and flow, filled her with anticipation, and affirmed her identity as part of a big, glamorous, and hospitable family.

It is not just that company events have replaced traditional holidays in my patients' lives. Holidays themselves are often spent at work. Given that so many of the people I see have turned to the workplace in part due to the absence of family, working on a holiday can be a highly coveted activity.

Ingrid routinely went to work on Christmas and New Year's. There, at one of the foremost bastions of the new economy, she found many of her coworkers talking, drinking, and playing games. She describes these times as thoroughly enjoyable and absorbing. She states that it never occurred to her to spend the holidays anywhere else. E-Stream was where she belonged. Grace often volunteered to work when her store was open on a holiday, because it drew her attention away from the fact that her children were absent, and she had no one with whom to celebrate. Sarah was exuberant when the division she worked for at PeoplePoint announced it would be open and sponsoring a potluck dinner on Thanksgiving. And, of course, Teri's enthusiasm for working on New Year's Eve is what initiated her growing self-awareness of her emotional dependence on her workplace.

Many corporations are cognizant of their role as replacement families. USAA Insurance in San Antonio bakes 5,000 pies on Thanksgiving for its employees and their families who eat at the company cafeteria on that day. Scitor in Sunnyvale, California; David Weekley Homes in Houston; and Micro-Strategy in Vienna, Virginia, have all taken their employees en masse on weeklong vacations to island resorts. Microsoft turns away employees on New Year's Eve because so many volunteer to work. Cisco Systems has stayed open because it "felt [that] leaving families, especially single-parent households to fend for themselves this New Year's Eve wasn't in keeping with the spirit of the season."

As CEOs talk about infusing the workplace with "emotional ties" and "love"; as management uses explicit and implicit references to embracing corporate "families"; as logos and branding pervade company cultures and employees' wardrobes; and as our most valued rituals, holidays, and celebrations increasingly are spent with coworkers rather than relatives, the workplace of the twenty-first century is becoming family and home to many in America.

WORK AS COMMUNITY

In 2000, Malcolm Gladwell described the new offices of an advertising agency:

> Two years ago, the advertising agency TBWA\Chiat\Day moved into new offices in Los Angeles. . . . The new office is an almost perfect embodiment of . . . community. The agency is in a huge old warehouse, three stories high and the size of three football fields. It is informally known as Advertising City, and that's what it is: a kind of artfully constructed urban neighborhood. The floor is bisected by a central corridor called Main Street, and in the center of the room is an open space, with cafe tables and a stand of ficus trees, called Central Park. There's a basketball court, a game room, and a bar. Most of the employees are in snug workstations known as nests, and the nests are grouped together in neighborhoods that radiate from Main Street like Paris arrondissements. The top executives are situated in the middle of the room. The desk belonging to the chairman and creative director of the company looks out on Central Park. The offices of the chief financial officer and media director abut the basketball court. . . . A small part of the building is

elevated above the main floor on a mezzanine, and if you stand there and watch the people wander about with their portable phones, and sit and chat in Central Park, and play basketball in the gym, and you feel on your shoulders the sun from the skylights and listen to the gentle buzz of human activity, it is quite possible to forget that you are looking at an office.

This kind of new-economy workplace remains unknown to most Americans, but it signals a direction in corporate ideology toward constructing replacement communities in geographic space, or at least in employees' imaginations. These "new company towns," as Jerry Useem describes them, can represent

thriving little civil societies: clubs for chess, genealogy, gardening, model airplanes, public speaking, tennis, karate, scuba diving, charity, and the like. At software maker SAS Institute in Cary, N.C., there's a breast cancer support group, a single parents' group, an international club that prepares foods of its members' native lands once a month, and a company-sponsored singing-and-dancing troupe called Vocal Motion. Downstairs at SAS, a troop of Brownies is busy decorating Christmas trees.

There's religion, too, in the form of on-site Bible study groups, which the Fellowship of Companies for Christ International numbers at 1,000 nationwide and growing fast.

While SAS Institute and TBWA\Chiat\Day clearly represent the cutting edge of the new economy workplace, they exist on a continuum of corporations that are self-consciously pro-

viding replacement community to their workers. Any trip to
the business section of the local bookstore or perusal of current
business magazines will reveal that building community at
work is regarded as necessary and beneficial. Michael Novak,
in his book *Business as a Calling,* asserts that "business builds
praiseworthy forms of community," and employers should "establish within the firm a sense of community. . . ."

Jay Conger, in *Spirit at Work,* claims that, due to the decline
of family and community, the workplace becomes "the essential area of life for us, and people consciously or unconsciously
bring their needs for community and spirituality to work."

As community that is based in geographic place or common
interests and shared purpose declines, community founded in
employment is what many Americans are turning to for a sense
of camaraderie, affiliation, and belonging. *It is where we socialize.* For working adults, more than two-thirds of all conversations during the day take place at work. Many studies have
shown that social connections with coworkers are the strongest
single predictor of job satisfaction. Simply put, employees with
friends at work are happier at work. *It is where we increasingly
satisfy needs previously met in neighborhoods.* If companies provide on-site restaurants and take-home meals, we don't have to
go to local grocery stores or restaurants. If there are company
gyms and sports teams, we don't have to join the neighborhood
gym or participate in local athletic leagues. If we can see the on-
site dentist, have our cars detailed in the employee parking lot,
or drop off our dry cleaning with the receptionist, work elimi-
nates running errands from our lives. And this makes sense.
With less time devoted to chores, we can spend more time at
work and be more productive employees. However, the demise
of the errand also removes one of our last reasons for connect-

ing with our neighborhoods, of meeting and having commerce with people who are not part of our workplace. In many ways then, *the workplace is offering a prefab life,* particularly for those who are searching for a means of anchoring themselves in a fragmented world.

In attempting to explain why people in their twenties are so enthusiastic about work in the new economy, twenty-something author Jordana Willner notes:

> Working all the time, though a seemingly noble symbol of in-dustrious maturity, is actually remarkably easy to do. Grown-up life is hard work, with responsibilities, obligations and conflicting demands. . . . If you work all the time at a com-pany that handles all the pesky details of outside life, life is a lot easier to handle. . . . Employees remain on-site, interacting with coworkers, likely having work-based conversations, but also having fun, being social, athletic and well-fed. . . .
>
> You get out of school, where you had a built-in peer group, you leave your parents' home, where you had auto-matic community, and you are suddenly on your own, frightened and without any obvious social path. Then along comes the opportunity to not only earn a living but also to step directly into a pre-fab life that includes friends, recre-ation, health care, services and parties.

Work is also where we increasingly receive public recognition. Corporations in the new economy seem more aware of people's needs for esteem, praise, attention, and recognition than virtu-ally any other sector of society does. Given the decreased oppor-tunities for the satisfaction of these needs and Americans' ensuing attention deficit, many employers fill these unmet desires through routinely having different forms of "recognition ceremonies," which encourage company loyalty, boost performance, and solidify corporate culture. Southwest Airlines leads corporate America in its emphasis on employee recognition:

> Winning Spirit Awards are given to folks who radiate the Southwest spirit. The Founder Award is given to someone who consistently goes beyond the call of duty. The President's Award is given to individuals who demonstrate Southwest's virtues and values, among others compassion for customers and coworkers, willingness to learn, embracing change, and spreading a sense of humor and fun. A Special Leadership Award is bestowed on someone who exemplifies the principles of the company's mission. Other awards include Community Relations Awards, a Good Neighbor Award, a Sense of Humor Award, and a Positively Outrageous Customer Service Award. A "top wrench" program is used to recognize mechanics, a "top cleaner" program to recognize plane cleaners.

I became acutely aware of the role of corporate recognition ceremonies in the lives of employees upon meeting Lin, a beautiful Vietnamese woman in her late thirties who was laid off from her job at the beginning of 2001. She had worked in a large financial institution in San Francisco, which she always refers to as "my company." I think it is possible to say that Lin had become addicted to recognition ceremonies.

Lin immigrated to the United States along with her mother and two brothers when she was fourteen. In order to help support her family, she lied about her age when she applied for a job through a Vietnamese support services group that aided recent immigrants in finding employment. She was hired by "my company," as a file clerk at minimum wage. Because of her youth, her profound sense of dislocation, and her utter determination to absorb American ways, Lin bound herself emotionally, almost spiritually, to her employer. She internalized its company culture as gospel. She set out to climb its corporate hierarchy with relentless determination. For Lin, "my company" was America, opportunity, a future, freedom.

Because of her innate intelligence and her resolve, Lin succeeded in getting promotions, commanding higher salaries, and greater responsibilities. After a number of years, the division for which she worked initiated a Most Valuable Employee of the Year Award along with other, lesser awards, to be given at the company's annual convention. Lin set forth to win this award through working tirelessly, often putting in sixty to eighty hours per week at her job. She would never take a break, never delegated any work that she absolutely didn't have to, and made a point of being endlessly cheerful, upbeat, and passionately devoted to the company values of "delighting customers," and "openness to continual improvement."

The happiest day of her life came for Lin when she succeeded in winning the Most Valuable Employee award. She was told that a private plane would take her and her family to the company convention being held about 100 miles south of San Francisco, that she would spend the night in a luxury hotel, and that she would receive the award at a formal dinner at an exclusive country club. Lin promptly spent $800 on a dress for the occasion. Her family was ecstatic and her coworkers, managers, and supervisees were highly laudatory.

The night of the awards ceremony remains vividly etched in Lin's memory:

Every eye was on me as I walked up to the stage. I walked real slow so I could see who was there and they could see me. I felt like I was walking through a sea of love. I didn't want to leave the stage because it felt so good. It was the best feeling to be treated like that.

The experience of being the center of attention, highly praised for what she did, who she was, and how she looked, was gratifying to Lin in a way nothing else in her life had been. All of these idealized men and women, the backbone of "my company," thinking only of her at that moment, filled her with a pride and a sense of wholeness and value that she seems to have craved. And after it was over and she settled back in the routine of her life, she only wanted to feel that sense again. So Lin dedicated her life to winning that award. She desired nothing more than to be recognized by the company that provided her with both a life and a lifestyle that allowed her to feel accepted, valued, and loved.

Lin won the award three years in a row. After her third award, she was told by management that the company needed to reward others. For the next two years, coworkers won the award. Throughout these years Lin continued to put forth the same effort, working in dramatic excess of what was expected, as she knew she was still regarded by "my company" as its most valuable employee. She states that she knew this in her heart. And, given that she received raises and bonuses throughout this period, her feeling was probably merited. For the two years that she did not receive the award, Lin was invited to sit at the dais at the annual convention dinner in light of her stature as three-time winner of the Most Valuable Employee award. This allowed Lin to feel like a queen.

In 2000, Lin won the award again. She states that she had hoped for this but thought it was out of reach, given "my company's" emphasis, as she states, "on being fair to everyone and letting different people win the award." This time, she spent over $1000 on her dress and hired a video cameraman to film her acceptance speech. When Lin told the women in the psychotherapy group that she had done this, she was asked by all to bring the video so we could witness the event she spoke about with such pride. Lin was clearly delighted with this request and brought the video the following week.

As I watched Lin first appear in the film, I found her almost unrecognizable. She was wearing so much makeup and her hair was so elaborately done and her dress so theatrical that, to me, she looked more like a fictional queen than a valuable employee. She walked remarkably slowly from her seat to the dais, smiling beatifically at the dinner guests she passed. Upon reaching the stage, she looked directly at the video camera, clearly performing to those she imagined would be watching this event on tape. As the president of her division was praising her, she fluttered her eyelashes. And, upon receiving the award, she again turned to the camera and delivered an acceptance speech that seemed to have been lifted directly from the Academy Awards and memorized precisely. She began by thanking "all the people who made this award possible." She then thanked her family and, most important, all the people at work who had demonstrated that "even the humblest people on earth can be truly rewarded." As she returned to her seat, carrying her award in her arms and turning her head slowly from side to side, soaking up the sea of love around her, her demeanor transported me back to the Miss America and Miss Universe pageants I had watched on television as a child. Perhaps Lin had watched these too.

Given all of this recognition, attention, praise, and love, Lin was emotionally devastated when she was laid off in the financial downturns of early 2001. Her division was reorganized due to an unexpected fall in profits, and her position was eliminated. To say that Lin never anticipated this does not quite capture her experience. In group it is not uncommon for Lin to sob and in a voice choking on tears rhetorically ask: "Did I think the ground under my feet could go away? Did I think the earth would stop turning? I was a four-time winner!"

When she was severed from the company for which she had worked forty to eighty hours per week for more than twenty years, the glue that held Lin's self together suddenly desiccated. For the past six years, Lin had given up virtually everything outside her job in order to demonstrate her status as most valuable employee. She craved the recognition and love she felt as a result of this status. There was no single person at her workplace that filled her selfobject needs. Rather, the entire company formed a self-defining and self-sustaining environment that allowed Lin to feel cohesive and worthy. Within this environment, it was the annual recognition ceremony around which she structured her life. It was there that the company community acknowledged Lin and allowed her to feel like a queen, or best actress, or Miss Universe. "My company" was really the only community Lin had ever experienced.

WORK AS SOCIAL MOVEMENT

Something is happening and it affects us all. A global revolution is changing business, and business is changing the world. . . . The structure of the company is changing; relationships between companies are changing; the nature of work is changing; the definition of success is changing. The

result is a revolution as far-reaching as the Industrial
Revolution.

—ALAN WEBBER AND BILL TAYLOR,
FOUNDERS OF FAST COMPANY

In ancient times, the philosopher, the priest, or the soldier
found a sense of transcendent purpose in what they did. I can
imagine the Spartan soldier bleeding to death on the
battlefield and feeling, "My life is not a waste. I'm dying for
something bigger than myself." I mentioned this at a tech
conference not long ago, and a guy said, "That's the way I
want to feel about ecommerce solutions."

—DINESH D'SOUZA

The tens of thousands of Americans who have joined startups,
high tech, and biotech companies, and other leading sectors of
the new economy, often found something more than replacement family and community at work. For many, their jobs provided feelings of participating in a social movement, a sense
that they were changing history. Working with likeminded
coworkers, comrades in arms, to develop new forms of technology, pharmaceuticals, or entertainment allowed employees
to feel part of a world-historic transformation in how we live
our lives. The geographic and mythological locus of this movement has been, of course, Silicon Valley, a bland, suburban
landscape that became the epicenter of the new economy.

By car, by plane, they come. They just show up. They've
given up their lives elsewhere to come *here*. They come for
the tremendous opportunity, believing that in no other place
in the world right now can one person accomplish so much
with talent, initiative, and a good idea. . . . They come because it does not matter that they are young or left college

without a degree or have dark skin or speak with an accent. They come even if it is illegal to do so. They come because they feel that they will regret it the rest of their lives if they do not at least give it a try. They come to be part of history.

The allure that Po Bronson described spoke to both the actual place located in the Santa Clara Valley south of San Francisco, *and* the mythic quality of work as revolution, business as a form of history-altering activity that was a centerpiece of new economy ideology. Business magazines, such as the new economy's *Fast Company,* frequently heralded the new worker as a potential *change insurgent, business bolshevik,* or simply *revolutionary.* In that magazine's review of *Leading the Revolution,* a book by Gary Hamel, "the world's top business strategist," we were told that:

> You can become the author of your own destiny. You can look the future in the eye and say: I am no longer a captive to history. Whatever I can imagine, I can accomplish. I am no longer a vassal in a faceless bureaucracy. I am an activist, not a drone . . . I am a Revolutionary.

In numerous corporations that have seen themselves as changing the way business is done and, therefore, changing history, employees have been inducted into company cultures that inspire, exalt, ignite a sense of participation in something far grander than a job. Not infrequently, they have been presented with the heroic mission of their CEO or company founder, and swept up in a vision of their work that is filled with revolutionary zeal. A striking example of such a vision is that of Michael Saylor, CEO of MicroStrategy, a former software giant. After six weeks of training for new employees that the company refers to as *boot camp,* Saylor announces to the assembled: "Our mission is to make intelligence accessible everywhere. . . . Call some friends tonight, and ask what their company's mission is. Then ask yourself, Would I follow that organization to the ends of the earth? Or is it simply a place to spend forty hours a week?" Saylor closes his address by describing a bridge in Alcantara, Spain built by the Romans, and intended to stand forever: "We have the ability to turn the economy upside down, to enhance lives, and to drive the civilization forward—the same way that bridge was built to serve generation after generation. . . . You have the power to make us succeed or fail."

If one's job involves "driving civilization forward" and, therefore, requires a commitment to follow one's employer to the "ends of the earth," the workplace can become a pretty heady place. Where else can we feel so important, so inspired, so called to a higher moral purpose? I would argue that there is virtually no other place in American society today that invokes such heroism, that allows an average person to feel that he or she is a world-historic actor. Work assumes mythic proportions, the mantle of manifest destiny, and evokes altruism, courage, sacrifice, and, typically, awfully long hours. In the months following September 11, America evoked patriotism, intrepidity, and resolution with the slogan: "America: Open for Business." It is through our commerce, our dedication to our lives as economic actors, that we define ourselves as Americans and express our citizenship.

Ingrid is a striking example of someone who sees her employment as a revolutionary mission. E-Stream certainly functions as her family and community. It is where she spends all her time, including holidays, and where all her needs for companionship, recognition and a sense of belonging are met, but it is more than this. Ingrid's work represents a means of participating in a social movement. Like many revolutionary actors, Ingrid feels it is appropriate to sacrifice personal needs and desires in order to further the cause. It is only in light of believing that one is changing history that it becomes easy to work 110 hours a week and sleep on the conference-room floor. It seems to me that whenever Ingrid's commitment to total absorption in E-Stream begins to flag, she invokes her historic role:

> Oh, I don't know I just started feeling like maybe I need something else, some hobbies. . . . I used to ride horses as a kid and I was thinking "Why don't I do that anymore?" But then I started thinking about [a new product that E-Stream is developing] and I thought "Jesus, horses! You've got to be kidding. We're really gonna stir things up with this one." Literally everyone will know about this by next year, and you know, I'm part of it. I'm part of something really important here.

So, horseback riding—like having a relationship, or a family, or sex, or any interests beyond her job—is foreclosed, as work as social movement, business as revolution, is invoked and remembered.

This revolutionary perspective is nicely summarized in "Startups Revive Workers of the World," an op-ed piece written by David Sacks, a vice president of strategy at a dot.com:

> For many, joining a startup has become a declaration of independence from staid career tracks and a pledge of alle-

giance to a new ethos of entrepreneurship, self-confidence, and, most of all, courage. Driving them as much as the prospect of dot-com riches is the desire to live on the edge, to fight an epic battle, to experience in a very diluted way what previous generations must have felt as they prepared to go to war. But instead of violence, unbridled capitalism has become the preferred vehicle for channeling their energy, intellect and aggression . . .

Now is the time to join. The time to learn about yourself by living on the edge. The time to experience stakes unavailable at a professional firm or big company. If nothing else, you'll feel more alive.

I think this is exactly the point. There is little in our lives that allows us to feel truly alive, courageous, important. For young people in the 1960s and 1970s, participating in movements for free speech, civil and women's rights, and against the Vietnam War, provided a means of fighting an epic battle. American youth in the 1940s, going to war against fascism and supporting that war effort at home, got an enormous sense of being world-historic actors, of literally preserving democracy and combating evil. Today, those desires for meaning, purpose, and feeling alive are not served by religion, politics, or civic life. Increasingly, they are channeled into work, where so many of us feel more alive and therefore live more of our lives.

THE PROBLEM WITH EATING DOUGHNUTS

Inside the bleak and impersonal organization of Frederick Winslow Taylor, the workplace was not as pleasant, but the relationships of power and control were clear. Nothing much was required of the self, except to perform an assigned

function. . . . Taylor's pig-iron handler, "Schmitt," worked
under physical and mental constraints but did not have to
smile at the boss. He just had to move pig iron. Schmitt got his
self-esteem at home and in the marketplace. . . . He was the
economic man, the drinking man, and the ladies' man; but he
wasn't, and didn't have to be, the company man. There were
few or no social requirements to his job. He was not asked to
eat doughnuts with his coworkers and smile, or to talk about
his innermost feelings in company training seminars.

—JOANNE CIULLA

In so many ways, the new economy workplace is a more hu-
mane, more democratic, enlightened, and fun place to work than
the old way was. For a good proportion of its employees, opportunities for creativity and self-fulfillment remain great. For others, the new way becomes the only way, the only life they have.
For them, the replacement family and community, the shared
values and purpose, amenities, and references to organizational
democracy, caring, and love, are ends in themselves, not means
to goad them into working longer hours and more productively.
For them, their identities crumble when it is revealed that their
employer ultimately has to respect the bottom line over care, culture, or comforts. Their pain is often rooted in the contradiction
between what employers tell their employees they are doing, that
is, working together as a team, creating a family or community
where everyone's opinions are valued, promoting a shared purpose—and what they actually do—that is, lay off, demote, transfer, promote, and downsize based on the needs of shareholders
or venture capitalists, rather than those of employees. It is often
within this disjuncture that workers lose their way, cannot comprehend, blame themselves, or lash out in uncomprehending
rage. "I thought they cared." "What I had to say was supposed to
count." "They kept telling us we were a team."

Due to its emphasis on equality, culture, fun, and involvement, the new way obscures power relationships in a manner in which the old way did not. If those who controlled the company sat in luxurious corner offices and wore expensive suits, it was easier to immediately *see* power than if the CEO sits in a cubicle and wears shorts to work. If an employee parties with her supervisor and is repeatedly told that democratic teamwork is what drives the company's success, it is harder to comprehend layoffs and abuses of power than if there are firm boundaries between supervisors and supervisees. If we believe we are *associates* or *partners*—as employees at Wal-Mart, Amazon, LensCrafters, Marriott International, and Starbucks are called—we may forget that we do not call the shots. If amenities and social events are demonstrations of how much our employers care about us, it is shocking and wrenching to realize in an instant that they do not. If we are committed pigs, rather than involved chickens, we make ourselves more vulnerable to slaughter.

"Giving teams more control over their work schedules or job design is not the same as giving them the real clout needed to assert their own interests when they clash with those of shareholders or executives—as in the case of a corporate decision to downsize or contract out jobs," argues sociologist Charles Derber. "To presume that corporations and workers share a common good is to suggest that power is irrelevant."

The concept of power, the idea that employers and employees have antagonistic interests, is utterly absent from my patients' lexicons. One might say that their selfobject needs are so great that they are motivated to be naïve, to overlook power relationships in order to feel secure, connected, and acknowledged. However, I think theirs is not an entirely idiosyncratic world view. As a society, Americans often view business and its interests as representative of all our interests. With our long-standing distaste for the appellation *working class* in favor of the (incorrect) belief that most of us are *middle class,* coupled with the historic decline of unions, work in America has become more intensely personal rather than a collectively experienced phenomenon.

Unlike Western Europeans, Americans find little meaning in the concept of social class. Therefore, the idea of class antagonism or the unequal distribution of power finds little resonance. There is no context of meaning, no cognitive or theoretical tool to understand a betrayal at work. The plaintive cry, "I thought they cared," suggests a world in which we have only our own psyches and personalities to interpret relationships and events at work. According to Richard Sennett, employees' "sense of personal responsibility and personal guilt is compounded by the rhetoric of modern management, which attempts to disguise power in the new economy by making the worker believe he or she is a self-directing agent."

As a society, we seem to be more in love with business and place greater faith in its prerogatives than ever before. What is good for corporate America is good for Americans. And, because of the decline of family life, communities, labor unions, civic life, and trust in the authority of the state, there are simply no countervailing voices to question the power of business and faith in the market. Not only do we see corporate intervention as the answer to our social ills—to failing schools, overcrowded prisons, rising medical costs—but we view its transformation of the global economy as a benefit to us all.

This world view seeps into, and pervades, the workplace. It colors our faith in the corporations for which we work. It un-

derscores our fealty and our desire to believe in all the protestations of love, care, commitment, shared purpose, and the valuing of every employee's interests. If we are encouraged to
partake of corporate culture from both within and without the
workplace, the pull to believe in, identify with, idealize, and
sacrifice for, can envelop us. In the absence of any other invitations that feel similarly compelling, from any other social institutions that desire our participation in such an encouraging
way, many of us find not giving all of ourselves to our jobs a
difficult proposition. We are emotionally hungry, and the new
economy workplace feeds that hunger, fattens us up, and en-
courages us to be totally committed with the blessing of the
larger society in which we live.

CHAPTER FIVE

Why Women?

My mamma drilled into me that I should never trust a man.
"Be your own person," she'd say. "Put your trust in a job."
— LEATRICE JOHNSON,
U.S. POSTAL WORKER

OF THE NEARLY 200 PATIENTS that I have seen over the
past decade who have been married to their jobs, about 85 percent have been women. This gender asymmetry may speak to
the fact that, at any one time, two-thirds of psychotherapy patients in the United States are women. In general, women tend
to be more ready to seek help, more willing to admit to psychological distress, and more eager to explore feelings. However, I
believe that the gender imbalance in my caseload cannot be ac-
counted for merely by women's greater participation in psychotherapy. Instead, I would argue that women bring different
needs, interests, and ways of being into the workplace. They
are more likely to marry their jobs and, therefore, more inclined to feel betrayed when their employers reveal that they
don't care, aren't really a family, or that they value the bottom
line over corporate cultures built on so-called emotional ties
and love.

By listening to the ways in which my patients understand
and construct their lives, I am inclined to think that women

tend to marry their jobs at much higher rates than do men, both for psychological and economic reasons. While men clearly are susceptible to similar selfobject needs and can feel just as betrayed, in general, their very definitions of self and their relationship to the paid labor force allow them to be more emotionally resilient to offers of workplace matrimony.

SELF IN CONNECTION

When the average woman goes to work each morning, she enters her workplace with greater relational needs than her male counterpart. She typically will seek out friends, conversation, sharing, belonging, and reciprocity with people in her work environment that sustain a sense of self that is founded in connection with others. Although actual women exist along a continuum of relational capacities and needs, that continuum is organized around being able to make and then to maintain affiliations and relationships. Conversely, when the average man enters his workplace, he is more likely to seek out ways of defining himself through autonomy and emotional separateness from others. He may socialize on the job, but he is less likely to be searching for sustaining emotional connection with others in quite the same way.

Our understanding of how women tend to define themselves through attachment and relationship to others and men through autonomy and separation is most clearly explained by sociologist and psychoanalyst Nancy Chodorow in her highly influential book, *The Reproduction of Mothering*. It is here that we learn how women's primary responsibility for rearing children engenders different relational needs and ways of constructing selfhood in men and women.

In order to become masculine—that which is other than female—a son erects well-defined ego boundaries that firmly set him apart psychologically from the human being with whom he is originally bonded. This process allows the boy to develop a distinct sense of self and a need for relationship to others that respects the autonomy of the self. Any close, interpersonal relationship that begins to resemble the union or symbiotic character of the early mother–son bond carries within it a threat to a masculinity that is primarily founded in opposition to the maternal.

Girls, on the other hand, develop their sense of self in *relation* to the mother, not *opposition*. Because they are mothered by someone of the same gender, girls' process of separation from the mother retains a greater sense of connection and continuity than that which exists between mother and son. Daughters, therefore, develop more fluid or permeable ego boundaries than sons and a greater tendency to define themselves, to find their identity, in relationship to others. Their relational needs are centered on maintaining feelings of closeness and contact with others, largely because they never had to deny the original bond with their mother in order to form their selves and their basic sense of femininity. As Chodorow asserts, girls develop

> with a basis for "empathy" built into their primary definition of self in a way that boys do not. Girls emerge with a stronger basis for experiencing another's needs or feelings as one's own. . . . [W]omen remain preoccupied with ongoing relational issues in a way that men do not. . . . Masculine personality, then, comes to be defined more in terms of denial of relation and connection, whereas feminine personality comes to include a fundamental definition of self in relationship.

While there certainly is enormous variation around these ideal types, in general, women seem to have greater concern about hurting others' feelings and being hurt emotionally than men do; they have more intense friendships; a greater preoccupation with issues of personal inclusion and exclusion; a greater need for ongoing connection to others; a stronger desire for sharing and mutuality; and more ambivalence and conflict over success, achievement, and competition. Conversely, men generally feel more threatened by intimacy; are less attentive to feelings and emotions; more apt to feel their masculinity challenged by insufficient respect, acknowledgment, and deference from others; and experience greater comfort in acting autonomously and competitively.

These psychological differences typically render women more social than men, and more concerned about caring and being cared for by others. On virtually every empirical indicator of social connectedness—from long-distance phone calls to family and friends, the exchanging of greeting cards and gifts, time spent visiting with friends, frequency of volunteer work, or the amount of time spent engaged in informal conversation—women surpass men.

Women's greater need for defining themselves through connection with others follows them into the workplace. As they spend more time on the job, and less time at home or in their neighborhoods and communities, women are bound to seek out feelings of closeness, connection, and caring from those they spend the majority of their days with, that is, their supervisors and coworkers. The cases of Grace and Michelle illustrate this well.

As we saw in chapter 2, Grace left her job after feeling betrayed by her supervisor, Tanya. Tanya's perfidy did not stem

from anything directly related to the job or to Grace's performance but, rather, from her inattention to Grace's medical con-
dition. Tanya, to whom Grace looked for friendship, closeness,
and sharing, did not seem to empathize with her supervisee's
fears and anxieties about her impending surgery. Grace looked
to Tanya and her coworkers for emotional support, feelings of
mutuality, and care. She experienced profound disappointment
when her supervisor asked her to work overtime after returning from a doctor's appointment. Tanya revealed herself to be
more concerned about the staffing needs at the supermarket
than Grace's personal travails.

In similar fashion, Michelle formed an intense attachment
to her supervisor, Shelby. Her relationship to Shelby was the
linchpin that wedded her to her job in a deeply devotional
state. Her overriding desire for defining herself through connection with others propelled Michelle to marry her job at the
import–export business, then to remarry the corporation that
hired her in Silicon Valley.

Another example of how women's relational needs can suf-
fuse their experience in the workplace is illuminated by the
case of Bea, who has been a member of one of my groups for almost three years. At age sixty-three, Bea came to see me after
working as a receptionist in an obstetrics-gynecology practice
for almost twenty years. Bea was clear and concise in describing why she could no longer work at the job she loved: "I got
sick of never being invited to eat lunch with the other girls."

Over the course of her tenure at work, Bea had seen many
of the office staff come and go. The last five years at her job
brought with them a staff that did not seem to like her, for totally unclear reasons. Perhaps it was her age, her zealous de-
fense of the doctors whenever a dispute arose between them

and an administrative staff member, or the hours she worked in excess of what was expected of her. She wasn't sure, but she was never asked to go to lunch with the other support staff.

Bea tried to cope with this sense of exclusion in a variety of ways. She brought in treats for her coworkers. She gladly covered for them when they had to be away from the office. She took walks on her lunch break rather than eat by herself. She spent significant amounts of time crying in the office bathroom. She talked endlessly to her husband, adult children, and friends about the situation. Finally, she pleaded with the senior gynecologist to intervene for her with the staff. When he refused this request, telling her that he couldn't get involved in this level of "pettiness," Bea felt defeated and heartbroken. "I tried everything to make them like me. I literally rolled over backward. I know if I went there one more day, any piece of self-esteem I had left would have crumbled."

I believe that Bea's reason for leaving a job she loved would be at least suspect and most likely incomprehensible to most men. To them, feeling such a profound sense of rejection and personal failure over being excluded from lunch would certainly seem petty, and many women would share in this assessment. My guess, however, is that most women could identify with some version of Bea's plight. Perhaps her utter lack of guile, her ingenuousness would make many women uncomfortable, but her concern about having friends, being included, being liked and connected to others pervades most women's experience. It is an experience that can tether them to coworkers and supervisors, often wedding them to their jobs.

As more and more women work in the paid labor force, coworkers replace neighbors and extended family members in providing emotional connection, conversation, gossip, and sharing. Bea's experience upon quitting her job highlights this shift in women's lives from neighborhood to workplace.

Bea married in 1957 and had her first child in 1959. She still lives in the same house that she and her husband purchased forty-one years ago. Bea was a full-time homemaker and mother until going to work for the gynecologists' office when her youngest child was in high school. She states that it was not until she quit her job three years ago that she became fully aware of how much her neighborhood has changed over the course of the past twenty years:

> When I was raising my kids, everyone else was too, so there was always someone you could talk to, borrow things from, that type of the thing. . . . Yes, I knew my neighbors very well because we were all home during the day, all had husbands that worked. We were all just trying to get by. . . . And now it feels kind of sad that the neighborhood feels so different. People don't help each other out anymore. Everyone's on their own it seems. . . . When I take my walk [in the morning] it's like a ghost town because everyone works. . . .

Bea's desire to live her life surrounded by others who provide companionship and connection has now been thwarted by the world of work. Feeling as though she has failed in making her workplace a community or neighborhood, she encounters her real neighborhood, a place that is now devoid of people. Once alive with stay-at-home moms, their children, and their mutual needs and concerns, Bea's community has been transformed by the demands of the workplace that now control most women's lives. Feeling that she is too old to start at a new job, Bea searches for other arenas outside of work for friends and a sense of belonging. She walks the streets of her neighborhood during the day to find a ghost town. She has continued to come to group for over three years, not so much because she needs therapy but because she desires connection to other women: "I can't imagine stopping," she says. "I love to hear the stories and see how everyone's doing every week." In other words, group therapy serves some of the functions of Bea's neighborhood circa 1960. It allows her to share and gossip and immerse herself in others' lives, their travails and successes. It may be a diluted form of community, but it speaks to an ongoing need to sustain her sense of self through ongoing connection with others.

SINGLEHOOD AS THE STATE OF AFFAIRS

For women, in particular, to take a job is often today to take out an emotional insurance policy on the uncertainties of home life.
                                                    — ARLIE HOCHSCHILD

Whenever women marry, they often do so not just for emotional reasons. Throughout history, women have married for economic survival and security. Thus, when women today marry their jobs, a similar logic applies. In a world of rapid economic change, family disintegration, and the ongoing expectation that it is women's responsibility to rear children, many, if not most, women look to the workplace for economic survival and security. Many are putting their hopes for fidelity and commitment through sickness and in health, for richer or poorer, in their employers. Jobs, not men, seem to offer more in the way of economic stability over the long haul.

As described in chapter 2, most women face the prospect of

having to support themselves—and, often, their children—for increasing parts of their lives. Due to divorce, the later age of marriage, and vast increases in out-of-wedlock childbirth, only 23.5 percent of households today are composed of a married couple with children. Given that 40 percent of adult women are single, and that the marriage rate has fallen one-third for women since 1970, Barbara Dafoe Whitehead, co-director of the National Marriage Project at Rutgers University, concludes: "The reality is that marriage is now the interlude and singlehood the state of affairs."

Singleness *per se* is not enough to propel women to marry their jobs more often than men do. What differentiates women's experience economically from men's is twofold: They continue to be responsible for rearing children, and they do so in a labor market that pays them less than men. Barbara Ehrenreich summarizes this state of affairs concisely:

> For women as a group, the future holds terrifying insecurity: We are increasingly dependent on our own resources, but in a society and an economy that never intended to admit us as independent persons, much less as breadwinners for others.

Today, one-third of all children are born to unwed mothers, compared to 5 percent in 1950. Although some of this increase is due to unmarried couples cohabiting, it is unequivocally true that women face the prospect of rearing children on their own for some part of their lives in an historically unprecedented fashion. Just since 1990, the number of families headed by single women has increased 25 percent. Although single fatherhood has increased during the decade as well, such households represent only one-sixth of all single parent homes. With divorce rates remaining relatively constant, and mothers continuing to be the ones typically awarded custody, what Barbara Ehrenreich stated in 1983 holds true today: "The result of divorce, in an overwhelming number of cases, is that men become singles and women become single mothers."

Due to a labor market that pays women less and that privileges full-time employment, single mothers are at a huge economic disadvantage. When women work full time, their median weekly wage is only 76 percent that of men. Given that women, particularly single mothers, constitute a greater share of the part-time and contingent workforce, their earning capacities are even more limited. This economic inequality ends up accounting for the fact that almost 40 percent of all unmarried mothers are earning less than what's needed to buy themselves and their children adequate nutrition, clothing, and shelter.

In many ways, then, the great historical collision of the latter part of the twentieth century has been between the enormous changes in women's lives and the unchanging quality of our social conventions. Child rearing continues to be virtually the exclusive responsibility of women but, due to the decline of both the family wage and the permanence of marriage, they are increasingly parenting alone. They are doing so in an economic and social order that pays them less, does not provide affordable and quality child care, penalizes them for taking time off and for working part time, and, increasingly, restricts any kind of state support to women with dependent children.

The new economy offers both women and men an environment of risk and insecurity. In the absence of anchoring institutions, we are advised to depend only on ourselves, our ability to promote and market the brand called *You.* However, in this geography of constant uncertainty, men and women are not created equal. Given their handicap, it is unsurprising that women might cling a little bit more to an institution that promises steady income, a sense of solidity and belonging, and a ready-made group of potential friends. With the historical demise of the lifelong, wage-earning husband, the workplace offers many women their best chance at some modicum of economic security. That many of them marry their jobs in response to this offer can be understood in light of the economic dilemmas they face.

Of all the women patients I have met with over the course of the past ten years, Leatrice has been the clearest in her choice of a job over a man to provide her with security. She traces the origins of this stance to the experience of her mother, a figure about whom she often speaks in reverential tones. Leatrice's father abandoned his wife when Leatrice was in the womb:

> At six months' pregnant he just took off. No word, no note, no nothin'. So there she was, hadn't even graduated from high school. No skills, nothin'. And her mother, oh boy. She thought my mamma was a hellion for getting married in the first place. She wouldn't even let her move back home. "You think you so grown up, you figure out what to do." You know, that kind of thing. So my mamma says "all right" and she gets herself a place to live and a job and she has me and she does fine.

Leatrice's mother pieced together a life and raised her daughter never to trust a man, never to indulge in romantic fantasies, and to believe in hard work and a steady job as security and salvation. As Leatrice tells it, work never let her mother down. It may have paid poorly, but it was always there in some form, allowing a single mother to raise a daughter without help from kin or the state.

Thus, when Leatrice graduated high school—with honors—she decided to find a job that she believed would offer her the greatest security. Within two months of graduation, she was hired by the U.S. Postal Service as a mail batcher. She received excellent pay and benefits. She developed a wide circle of friends within the post office and describes having a life that was without a care in the world. Leatrice continued living with her mother and had a number of boyfriends, but she never once considered marriage or living with one of the men with whom she was involved. "I was raised to be my own person. I like myself. I don't need some man telling me what to do, waiting on him, 'could you get me a beer' after I been working all day."

When she was twenty-three, Leatrice gave birth to a daughter, and states that she never considered marrying her child's father, a postal worker, nor allowing him to have anything more than weekly visits with their daughter. Seven years later, she had another child, a son, with another boyfriend and adopted the same stance. Throughout these years, Leatrice worked steadily and was able to have her children cared for by working the night shift, so that she could be with them during the day and her mother could look after them at night.

At age twenty, Leatrice's daughter moved out of the house to go to college. One month later, Leatrice's mother was diagnosed with stomach cancer, and she died within the year. This was an extremely difficult time for Leatrice, as her mother had been so central to her life, and her daughter had been a real joy to have at home. Leatrice states that she missed them both enormously and found herself volunteering to work overtime in order to keep herself busy.

It was during this time of working fifty-hour weeks that Leatrice began experiencing pain in her hands, wrists, and forearms. After many visits to the doctor, she was diagnosed with bilateral carpal tunnel syndrome. She wore braces on both wrists and was able to continue working, as they gave her some relief. However, the pain worsened and, at age forty-nine, Leatrice was forced to stop working. She filed a Workers' Compensation claim, as she believed that the carpal tunnel was clearly a repetitive stress injury caused by her job. Thus Leatrice was astounded when the Post Office denied her claim. Perhaps astounded does not quite capture what she felt.

I mean, this was too much! I gave them my life and they tell me it's not their fault! So I march down there and I say "this must be a mistake; this can't be right." And they say, "Leatrice, this is what it says. You can appeal it, blah, blah, blah." And I think this is it, I'm gonna kill myself. So I go home and I tell my son "I'm gonna kill myself" 'cause there's no way that I'm gonna accept this. I gave them my life. And I'm crying and my son thinks I'm goin' crazy. . . . So he calls the police. My son calls the police, and they come and they take me to the loony bin and lock me up as "a danger to myself."

Leatrice spent three days in an inpatient psychiatric unit. She was placed on antidepressant medication, and sent home with a referral to a therapist in the group practice for which I work. After meeting with this therapist for about two months, Leatrice was referred to one of my groups.

When she first came to group, Leatrice appeared to be in a state of shock. She still hadn't assimilated the Post Office's betrayal. Her faith in employment as salvation had been a bedrock in her life, a belief system that appeared to have almost religious underpinnings. As chronic, physical pain became her daily companion, she was continuously reminded of how the Post Office saw her as expendable. "Now that I can't do my job, they treat me like garbage. . . . I gave them the best years of my life and what do they care that my hands hurt all the time?" The economic reality that Leatrice now has to face is that the Post Office offers no disability compensation; once she uses up her sick days she will have no income.

Incredulously, Leatrice asks the group, "So where do you turn? Who can you trust?" Having absorbed her mother's distrust of men and marriage, Leatrice avowed that to be both independent and secure as a woman it was necessary to invest in work. She followed this article of faith. She married her job for largely economic reasons and, at age forty-nine, finds herself deserted in much the same way as her mother was forty-nine years ago.

Bringing the Second Shift to Work

It is often assumed that the dramatic rise in women's labor force participation over the last thirty years has prompted women to approach the world of work in a fashion similar to that of men—thinking of their own needs, of how to get ahead, how to break the glass ceiling. Certainly, the business-advice literature of the new economy calling for change insurgency and free-agent nations makes no distinction between the interests of men and women. However, many of the women I see

who have married their jobs have done so through transforming the workplace into homelike environments, into sites
where more traditional wifely roles and duties are enacted.

Rather than accepting definitions of paid work as an inherently cold, contractual obligation, they implicitly or unconsciously bring with them into the workplace some version of
familism or, the second shift.* By so doing they are approaching
the workplace quite differently from their male coworkers.

In their book, *The Minimal Family,* Jan Dizard and Howard
Gadlin define *familism* as "a reciprocal sense of commitment,
sharing, cooperation, and intimacy" embedded in "both material and emotional dependency and obligation. . . . Familism
embraces solicitude, unconditional love, personal loyalty, and
willingness to sacrifice for others."

Interestingly, they argue that familism does not have to reside within the family. They point out that in colonial America,
familism characterized both family *and* community life, but began to exist exclusively within the family only in the nineteenth
century:

> Most Americans are so accustomed to distinguishing be-
> tween family and nonfamily relationships that the differ-
> ence seems a natural one to them. But while the significance
> of family ties has long been acknowledged, the distinct sepa-
> ration of family and public spheres is a relatively new dis-
> tinction. . . .
> [A]s familism was progressively squeezed out of public
> life by the spread of marketplace rationality . . . familism

---

*Ana Villalobos originally suggested to me that women bring familism
with them into the workplace.

came to be associated almost exclusively with the family. The world outside the home might be uncaring, immoral, and viciously competitive, but the family at least was a place where cooperativeness, mutual concern, and morality could safely reside.

In *The Second Shift,* sociologist Arlie Hochschild demonstrates how so many working women today have two work shifts: their paid job and their unpaid job, doing housework and child care. She calculates that due to these two shifts, "women worked roughly fifteen hours longer each week than men. Over a year, they worked an extra month of twenty-four-hour days a year." She concludes:

> Most women without children spend much more time than men on housework; with children, they devote more time to both housework and child care. Just as there is a wage gap between men and women in the workplace, there is a "leisure gap" between them at home. Most women work one shift at the office or factory and a "second shift" at home.

After many years of running groups for women who married their jobs, I came to realize that part of their implicit marriage contracts was founded in a willingness, actually an eagerness, to infuse the workplace with familism and the second shift. Many women seemed to refuse to leave commitment, sharing, cooperation, material and emotional obligation, personal loyalty, and a willingness to sacrifice for others at home. They transported these qualities into the workplace. Surprisingly, they also brought with them aspects of the second shift.

In the mid-1990s, one of my psychotherapy groups began

calling itself "the muffin club." They assumed this identity when they realized that each of the eight members had routinely brought bagels or muffins, which they purchased with their own money and at their own initiative, to work. As the women became more open and self-revealing in group, they began sharing all the ways in which they brought the second shift to work. Office cleanliness emerged as a significant topic of conversation. Most of them found aspects of their workplaces' janitorial services substandard and took it upon themselves to vacuum, dust, wash kitchen sinks, and clean the toilets. Many of them brought in their own cleaning supplies. In one particular session, each of the women discussed the amount of time she spent each week thinking about what treats to bring to work (e.g., muffins, candy, bagels) and how best to supply them. Should she go to Costco and get the most muffins for the least amount of money? Or should she buy from the local bakery, spending more money but providing better muffins? Perhaps people were getting sick of muffins. Maybe she should bring in bagels this week. Or, maybe she should just spend the time baking. People always preferred home-baked goods. But bagels were less fattening and when was she going to find time to bake anyway? Cleaning and supplying food for coworkers were clearly not part of these women's job descriptions, but they nonetheless assumed these tasks as an intrinsic part of their work lives.

Similarly, they and so many other women I have seen enacted rituals of familism throughout their work week. They organized celebrations of coworkers' and supervisors' birthdays, and circulated greeting cards acknowledging births, deaths, anniversaries, children's graduations, and promotions.

They often brought coworkers videotapes of TV programs, exchanged CDs, baby clothes, and recipes. They organized office potlucks, parties, and off-site get-togethers. They gossiped, listened to others' problems, and often continued workplace conversations on e-mail or the telephone at night or over the weekend. They frequently ran errands for their bosses—picking up dry cleaning, walking dogs, housesitting, buying food. It is through these acts that they demonstrated care, obligation, loyalty, reciprocity, solicitude, and a willingness to sacrifice for others. One could also say that these acts represented expressions of their marital vows.

In bringing familism and the second shift to work, my patients are making their workplaces more homey, more familiar, more *female,* insofar as women have been historically identified with domesticity. In part, they are responding to the very recent and dramatic transformation in women's lives whereby full-time, lifelong work in the paid labor force has become the rule rather than the exception. They are implicitly creating ways of working that incorporate values and practices founded in the home. Often only a single generation away from mothers who had identities exclusively constructed around domesticity, my patients are blurring the distinctions between home and work, private and public.

Arlie Hochschild notes that today "many women of every social class and in every kind of job are faced with a common problem: 'how shall I preserve the domestic culture of my mother and grandmother in the age of the nine-to-five or eight-to-six job?'" She concludes that women accomplish this through the second shift: "On weekends and holidays most working women revert to being housewives . . . battl[ing] to carry forward a domestic culture—a culture of homemade apple pie, home-sewn Halloween costumes, hand-ironed shirts."

I would argue that, since Hochschild made this observation in 1989, fewer women have the opportunity to revert to being housewives. With the increasing hours spent at work and the decreasing investment in home as anything more than a refueling station, many women are attempting to preserve domestic culture through bringing that culture to work with them each morning. Rather than carrying on their mothers' and grandmothers' traditions at home, they are baking homemade apple pie for their coworkers (like Michelle), orchestrating company Halloween pumpkin-carving contests (like Sarah), and picking up hand-ironed shirts at the cleaners for their boss (like Brenda).

Beginning in the second half of the eighteenth century and continuing throughout the nineteenth, men left farms for factories, offices, the city. Due to industrialization they were cut off from domesticity, a sphere that became the province of women alone. As work life became more alienated, more competitive, anonymous, and contractual, the home emerged as a haven in a heartless world. And, it was women who preserved this haven, who preserved "an orientation toward life that was closer to what had been," as Arlie Hochschild points out. Through protecting and maintaining values and practices founded in an agrarian way of life, women ideally provided their husbands and sons with a buffer, a respite from the new, heartless world that increasingly enveloped their lives.

Today, women in the workplace are encountering a world that is based in autonomy, competition, and the marketing of the self. In order to cope with this transition, many women are bringing with them into their jobs an orientation toward life that is closer to what has been. They are transporting familism and elements of the second shift into their jobs, making the workplace more domestic, more caring, and providing themselves and their coworkers and supervisors with a buffer, as so many of us move from living at home to living at work.

While it is certainly possible to romanticize these acts and recognize the ways in which my patients' second shift activities benefit the workplace, it is important also to recognize that familism and the new economic order are fundamentally at loggerheads. A system founded in profit maximization, competition, contractual relationships, and continual risk and change, is antithetical to the loyalty, obligation, cooperation, and sacrifice by which *familism* is defined. Due to this basic opposition, women who attempt to make the workplace a domestic arena founded in reciprocity and care are ultimately opening themselves to emotional betrayal. Bringing the second shift to work fosters marrying the job, and puts women at a potential disadvantage.

When Sarah, a leading member of the muffin club, volunteered to orchestrate office parties and celebrations of staff members' birthdays; when Michelle brought in homemade baked goods every Monday; when Bea offered to cover any coworker's shift; or when Brenda walked her boss's dog, I believe that management, and even some coworkers, thought less of them on some level. Because their acts and ways of being in the workplace identified them with more domestic, feminine, or maternal qualities, they represented something attractive on the one hand, and anachronistic and diminished on the other. Certainly they were sought out by coworkers for companionship and support, and by supervisors for extra work and personal favors, but I believe they were also taken for granted, as most maternal figures are. Their care was seen as unconditional, offered perhaps too freely. The fact that they seemed so eager to please made them vulnerable to exploitation. Their acting out of more traditional feminine roles seemed to make some other women in their workplaces uneasy. After about six months in group, Bea saw this clearly in regard to her own experience with the other staff members in her office. She said, "I think these girls thought maybe I was too much like their mother. My daughter was telling me that these days you go to work and want to be equal to men and maybe they saw me as catering too much [to the all-male physician staff]."

In today's workplace, to be too identified with a traditional female role is tantamount to not being taken seriously, diminishing one's chances for advancement and achievement in a work world defined in opposition to familism. Therefore, as much as my patients made their workplaces more homey and comfortable, their activities evoked ambivalence, an ambivalence that I believe is rooted in our conflicts over dependence and autonomy. In bringing familism to work, they highlight a predicament succinctly illustrated on the cover of *True* magazine for November 1970 and summarized by Arlie Hochschild:

> [A] commuter train is filled with businessmen reading morning newspapers and office memos. A bewildered middle-aged housewife in bathrobe and furry slippers, hair in curlers, searches the aisles for her husband, his forgotten briefcase in hand. Her husband is hiding behind his seat, embarrassed that his wife looks so ridiculous, so out of place. In

their suits, holding their memo pads, reading their newspapers, the men of the commuter car determine what is ridiculous. They represent the ways of the city; the housewife represents those of the peasant.

While Brenda, Sarah, Michelle, or Bea are clearly not housewives, their ways of being in the workplace can be viewed as *out of place,* in so far as familism and the second shift are identified with home. And, ultimately, *home* brings up issues of dependence, being cared for, bathrobes, furry slippers. Although few of us don suits to go to work these days, our T-shirts and jeans are not bathrobes. To some degree, we all must deny our needs to be cared for, to be dependent, in order to work. In this process of denial, many of us may not wish to be too closely identified with anything or anyone that reminds us of our dependency needs.

Thus, bringing familism and the second shift to work may be seen as having two possible outcomes. First, over time, it may actually transform the workplace. As people spend less time at home and more time on the job, the familism many women bring with them gradually may be incorporated into workplace practices. In some ways, this is already happening. Teamwork; recognition ceremonies; bringing pets to work; and caring amenities, such as free food, massage, and concierge services can be viewed as features of the new economy that piggyback on the culture that many women are bringing to work with them. In order to attract and retain female employees, who are expected to account for 48 percent of the workforce in the United States by 2005, employers simply may have to make their job environments more appealing to women. And, if we all continue to work longer hours than any industrialized nation on earth, both women and men's needs to have aspects of home transported to work may increase.

Conversely, bringing the second shift to work may back-fire—both for the individual women who attempt it and for the workplace in general. In the case of my patients, enacting familism at work typically obscures the distinctions between what is really home and what is work, between an ideal marriage based in mutuality, unfeigned care, and reciprocity, and so-called marriage to a job, which is based in inequality, power, and demonstrations of care that are implemented for instrumental reasons (i.e., attracting and retaining employees, and inducing them to work longer hours). Due to this obfuscation, my patients are astounded when they discover that their second shift efforts are not recognized or appreciated. They feel betrayed, unable to comprehend why their employers don't care. Often dwelling within their own cultures of familism, they are blind to the realities of the bottom line, rendered unable or unwilling to continue in their jobs.

Those of my patients who withdraw from the workforce take with them the contributions made by extremely hard-working, highly committed employees. Their departure not only negatively affects productivity, but diminishes the quality of workplace culture. Suddenly, there is no one organizing parties, or supplying muffins, or generously listening to a coworker's problem. Although they may be ambivalently regarded by some, for many, the familism my patients bring to work is sorely missed. This experience is clearly reflected in the reaction Bea encountered after quitting her job. The very staff members who excluded her from lunch sent her flowers and cards telling her how much they regretted her departure. The doctors she worked for implored her to return.

"Dr. B. [who told Bea her concerns were "petty"] called me maybe seven, eight times. He kept saying he didn't know how they'd get along without me. Was it more money, something he could do? But, you know, he had his chance, and I just wasn't interested anymore."

Changing Colors

Clearly, not all women respond to the demands of the workplace by attempting to import values and practices founded in domesticity. An altogether different strategy, among others, is to sever one's ties to familism and the second shift altogether. By eschewing all that is connected to home, one is free to devote oneself exclusively to the workplace.

Ingrid is an outstanding example of this strategy. As described in chapter 1, after earning her MBA, Ingrid worked for four years at one of the largest and best-established corporations in Silicon Valley. She then joined E-Stream, a startup that has since gone public and become wildly successful. When Ingrid began therapy with me she was thirty-nine, a vice president with literally no interests or human connection to speak of beyond her job. Ingrid's strategy for constructing a life at work has been to extinguish any attraction to the domestic, to familism, and to model herself as much as possible on the male corporate executive. This strategy has not been merely conscious and intentional but explicitly required by her job.

In 1987, when Ingrid took her first full-time corporate position at age twenty-seven, she was hired at the management level, earning almost $80,000 a year. Within the first six months, she was assigned a corporate coach to help her be more effective at the executive level of her company. The coach instructed her in a variety of matters: how to sit, for instance. Ingrid was told that she often appeared too eager, too anxious at meetings. Rather than leaning forward in her chair, she should always sit back, look relaxed, perhaps resting her arm on the back of the chair. Ingrid was also informed that her language needed improvement. She should eliminate the phrase "I feel" from her vocabulary and only use "I think." She should speak in short, declarative sentences. She should get to the point quickly, and convey a sense of certainty even if she were unsure. How she dressed was important, too. She should eschew pastels, most definitely pink, in favor of neutral tones that did not draw attention from her executive status. Any kind of emotional response was, of course, prohibited, and should be confined to the privacy of her office, out of the hearing range of coworkers.

Ingrid had not a moment of hesitation in adopting all these suggestions. In fact, she was ashamed that her employer felt the need to assign her a coach. This act led her to believe that her performance had been inadequate, that the way she presented herself was in some sense inferior to that of her coworkers. Surprisingly, it never seemed to cross her mind that almost all the people she worked with were men. Ingrid wanted nothing more than to fit in, be acceptable and accepted. She had landed one of the best positions of anyone in her graduating MBA class, and she wanted desperately to climb the corporate ladder. That she was in need of coaching because she was a woman, and not due to some individual fault, escaped her.

Over the course of once-, then twice-per-week, individual psychotherapy, Ingrid began to soften in her approach and reveal to me some of the problems that really drove her to seek help. She suffered from chronic insomnia and almost daily headaches. She had gastric problems that required her to take large quantities of antacids throughout the day. When she was driving, she found herself sometimes seized with the desire to career off the bridge she crossed twice a day. "What goes through your mind right before these episodes?" I would ask. "I don't know. Nothing," she would reply.

From session to session, I was never quite sure which Ingrid would walk through my door. At the beginning of our work together and continuing more sporadically throughout, the highly professional, emotionally defended, sarcastic, self-confident Ingrid would spend the hour regaling me with the amazing things that happened at work, the funny incidents, the times she had to take to task another VP or the CEO. In these sessions she was smug, triumphant, at the top of her game. On other days she would appear daunted, confused, despondent. Given her impressive salary and status, her challenging work, the house she owned outright, her BMW sports car, her flawless appearance and beautiful clothes, what did she have to complain about? When she would ask this question rhetorically, I would stifle the voice inside of me that wanted to reply "A life, you don't have a life!"

Ingrid had moved so far away from the world of emotions that she could not even identify what she had lost or what could be different. Because she had spent the past twelve years of her life married so completely to her job, she literally had no access to experiencing other ways of being. From the moment she was assigned a corporate coach, she developed the idea that her most basic features—the way she moved, looked, spoke—were faulty. These had to be changed or hidden. And, in the process of changing and hiding, Ingrid seemed to renounce not only her feminine ways of being in the world but any kind of domesticity. Her home became only a staging area where she prepared for, and recovered from, work. She lost virtually all connection to friends and family. And perhaps most tragically, she lost her awareness that these things mattered, that their absence lurked behind her insomnia, her stomachaches, her sudden, episodic desire to die.

Surely, Ingrid's situation is extreme, but I think it has more in common with that of women who bring the second shift to work than one might imagine. In her own way, Ingrid was motivated by a desire to please, to belong, that a number of women further down the corporate hierarchy, such as Michelle or Sarah, also evince. Ingrid's strategy is different due to a variety of factors: her class, education, and profession. She was also compelled by the first corporation for which she worked to adopt a male style and perspective. However, behind the coercion was Ingrid's desire to fit in and, because the environment to which she sought inclusion was so completely constructed around competition, autonomy, and the exclusion of feelings or of any remnant of the domestic, Ingrid really had no choice but to leave familism behind in order to succeed. That she did so in such a thorough manner caused her to exhibit a variety of psychosomatic symptoms. Unable to consciously acknowledge all that she had given up, Ingrid's body rebelled. At times, that wordless rebellion became so overwhelming that the only way to quell the conflict inside was to want to die, to drive off the bridge for reasons that she could not say.

Ingrid had buried her dependency needs, in a fashion more extreme than that of her male coworkers. They all had wives (many of them stay-at-home) or live-in girlfriends who undoubtedly buffered their experience of the harsher realities of corporate life. No matter how much the new economy workplace is more relaxed, fun, familylike, it eschews emotion and demands autonomy, self-assurance, risk taking, and flexibility at all levels but most certainly for its executives. Ingrid was at a disadvantage in this. Not only had her way of working set her apart, but she did not have a wife. She had no one in her life who was interested in the details of her life or her feelings. She was attempting the impossible. She was trying to make it in a man's world in a man's way but without the emotional and material support that men depend on to function effectively and "autonomously" at work.

The Problem That Has No Name, Revisited

> *Gradually I came to realize that the problem that has no name was shared by countless women in America. . . . For human suffering there is a reason; perhaps the reason has not been found because the right questions have not been asked, or pressed far enough. I do not accept the answer that there is no problem because American women have luxuries that women in other times and lands never dreamed of; part of the strange newness of the problem is that it cannot be understood in terms of the age-old material problems of man: poverty, sickness, hunger, cold.*
>
> —Betty Friedan

In 1963, Betty Friedan published *The Feminine Mystique,* a book that helped found the contemporary women's movement. In her trenchant investigation into the situation of women at the time, Friedan asserted that American women suffered from an unnamed malaise that expressed itself through such symptoms as psychosomatic complaints, undiagnosed depression, a reliance on tranquilizers, and/or a general disinterest in activities and responsibilities. Surprisingly, this problem was not the result of failing to achieve what constituted success as a woman. On the contrary, it seemed to define the lives of a large number of women who had lived up to the ultimate feminine ideal: They were suburban housewives and mothers who did not have to work, and could devote their lives to raising their children and tending to their husbands and homes. Friedan exposed these housewives' symptoms to be largely unspoken protestations against a confining definition of what it was to be a woman in mid-twentieth-century America. Compelled to put all of their energies and expressions of selfhood into their domestic roles, the 1950s and 1960s housewife "was afraid to ask even of herself the silent question—'Is this all?'"

In many ways, the problem that has no name can be thought of as a means of viewing any widely experienced social–psychological conflict that is expressed through a set of physical or behavioral symptoms but that remains outside of conscious awareness. Through this lens, the experience of the late-nineteenth century hysteric reflected a problem that had no name. While the seemingly wide-ranging, bizarre symptoms that many middle- and upper-class women displayed were lumped together under the term *hysteria,* the social etiology of these symptoms largely remained obscured. Instead, they were conceptualized narrowly as components of individual psychopathology. Because the hysteric—much like the mid-twentieth-century housewife—had often fulfilled society's expectations for what defined a successful woman, the *social* causes of her malaise remained hidden. Given that the problem ultimately resided in the most basic cultural definitions of what it was to be a woman, the hysteric and the doctors who treated her could not see the sources of her pain and symptoms. If she had succeeded in fulfilling her role—a role that was seen as natural—then her malaise had to reside within her psyche or physiology. The role itself was not open to examination.

Today, the woman who is married to her job can be seen as suffering from a problem that has no name. She is successful in that she not only works in the paid labor force—an expectation of all Americans—but she is extremely hard-working, dedicated, loyal, willing to go the extra mile, willing to sacrifice her own needs for those of her employer. In this sense she epitomizes the American valuation of work. So, when she develops symptoms—physical complaints, depression, panic attacks, suicidal thoughts, and so on—as a result of her job, such problems must be *her* problems.

When she comes to psychotherapy, she does not rail against the hegemony of work, nor the increasing expectation that we live at our jobs, nor the attention deficit that defines our harried lives. She comes with her symptoms in tow, a profound sense that she has failed, and a prevailing sense of confusion about what has happened to her. There seems to be no name for her problem. Why is she so upset? If she is successful, like Ingrid, there is no imaginable answer. If she is transferred to another, better-paying job, like Luba, any answer seems to make her look ungrateful. If her supervisor, like Grace's, doesn't express concern about her health, or her coworkers don't invite her to lunch, as with Bea, her answer makes her seem ridiculous. The expectation that she should work ceaselessly but with few institutional anchors, little care or attention and often no economic security is never raised. Because to work in such fashion, today, in the United States, is natural, God given.

Herein lies a question. Is our current work order, defined by the precepts of the new way, more congenial to men than to

women? As we have seen, the new economy demands an acceptance of flexibility, risk, and short-term commitment in
place of safety, security and long-term loyalty. Employees are
supposed to invest themselves completely in a job, then be able
to thoroughly disengage when the task is over. They are to rely
on themselves, the brand called You, and to welcome continuous change as not only inevitable but good. All of this is to be
accomplished without an economic or emotional safety net
from the state, extended family, or community. The change insurgent is a model of autonomy, able to function independently
in any environment, thinking only of how to work better,
smarter, faster. That such a person is typically conceptualized
in gender-neutral terms is reflected in Tom Peters' vision of the
new worker. According to Peters, one of the new economic order's most highly respected exponents:

> The world is going through more fundamental change than
> it has in hundreds, perhaps thousands of years. . . . Do you
> want to be a player, a full-scale participant who embraces
> change? Here is the opportunity to participate in the lovely,
> messy playground called "Let's reinvent the world."
> Here's a new role model I call Icon Woman:
> She is turned on by her work!
> The work matters!
> The work is cool!
> She is "in your face"!
> She is an adventurer!
> She is the CEO of her life!
> She is not God. She is not the Bionic Woman. She is
> determined to make a difference!

My Icon Woman, of course, embraces and exploits the Web.

She submits her resume on the Web and keeps it perpet-
ually active there. . . .

She creates and conducts scintillating projects on the
Web via a far-flung "virtual" stable of teammates
(most of whom she's never met). . . .

She is deeply committed to her self-designed, do-it-from-
anywhere-with-anybody "career" path. . . . Her only
security is her personal commitment to constant
growth and her global (virtual) rep for great work.

In this remarkable portrait of the twenty-first-century
worker, Peters fashions an action hero who embodies the excitement, liberation, and energy of the new economy *in extremis*. She
is certainly not dependent on anyone. Where she lives and with
whom is immaterial. Her only mission is exuberant change for
change's sake. It is unimaginable that this audacious, detached
humanoid could ever suffer self-doubt, much less any kind of
personal distress. Although we cannot take Icon Woman completely seriously, Peters's fantasy was not published in some obscure, on-line zine, but rather in *Time* magazine's cover story on
"Visions 21: Our Work, Our World." Icon Woman may not be
literal prediction but she is suggestive of qualities increasingly
expected of the twenty-first-century worker.

It is doubtful that many Americans would genuinely desire
Icon Woman's life, any more than people wish to become com-
puter-generated action figures. Yet the very exaggerations of
Icon Woman can serve to highlight many of the ideals of the
new economy. And as we observe these ideals, we can ask if
this "new role model," this iconic figure of the future is really a
woman after all. Or, is she more likely a man? Does Icon

Woman represent a fantasy that has more in common with men's ways of being in the world than women's?

It appears to me that Icon Woman does not have children and does not have any care-giving responsibilities whatsoever. In this sense, she represents the perfect American worker, in that she has *zero drag,* that is, no responsibilities beyond her work that would inhibit her from being continually "turned on by her work!" She seems to have no relational needs from her "stable of teammates—most of whom she's never met." She is autonomous, self-confident, assertive to the point of being "in your face!" And, she is utterly without need for any security. Her focus, her greatest need appears to rest in maintaining her "global rep for great work" and her "personal commitment to constant growth."

Is this a role model for most women? Given women's primary responsibility for rearing children and caring for those unable to care for themselves, can women be as free, as risk taking, as men in the new economy? Due to unequal pay and unequal opportunity, coupled with increasing rates of single motherhood, can most women disregard needs for security? Because so many women have second shifts or anticipate them, can they give themselves over to work, to being "full-scale participants who embrace change" in quite the same way as their less encumbered male counterparts? Are they really able to value autonomy and deny connection to others as Icon Woman appears to? Would most women feel satisfied having their "teammates" available to them only virtually? Given their ties to familism and the second shift, many, if not most, women come to the marketplace with far more drag than men. And I believe this makes a difference.

When I think about Brenda, Sarah, Luba, Marion, Grace, Michelle, Teri, Lin, and Bea, and their need for connection with others, for belonging, for being helpful, I cannot simultaneously think of Icon Woman. I can only imagine this "CEO of her life" having contempt for these women and their emotional needs. When I think of Ingrid, who comes closer to the Icon Woman model, I am aware of how much she denies her emotional needs in order to approximate the corporate executive ideal. In many ways Ingrid has learned to have contempt for her own needs.

If women do, in fact, have greater interests in emotional and economic security from their jobs, and a greater desire to find reciprocity, sharing, cooperation, and commitment at work than men do, are they at a disadvantage as the new economic order takes root? Do these different ways of engaging the workplace open them up to derision for not conforming to a model that is easier for men to achieve? Is part of the current problem that has no name women's own contempt for their difficulties in adapting to the new economy work environment?

These questions lead me to wonder if women's seemingly greater vulnerability to marrying their jobs is a reflection of a gender asymmetry in the new economy. Rather than being gender neutral or even having a woman as the iconic figure of the future, the emerging work order simply may be more hospitable to men. As Arlie Hochschild has pointed out, there "is a 'his' and 'hers' to the economic development of the United States." In keeping with this, I would suggest that women and men bring divergent psychological and economic needs with them to the workplace. Emerging from women's responsibility for child rearing, their unequal access to wages and job opportunities, and the decline of institutional anchors and safety nets, *her* new economy may be more challenging, more ominous than *his*. This is not to say that all men are having an easier time of it than all women. Rather, I am suggesting that on the continuum of *fit*—who better fits the requisites of the new economy— women may be more askew. It may be due to this misalign- ment, this disjuncture between many women's needs and the requirements of the new economy, that we face a twenty-first- century version of the problem that heretofore has had no name.

CHAPTER SIX

Living to Work or Working to Live

*Talk has always been the single most essential revolutionary
tool . . . People discussing, arguing, even fantasizing with
each other about what can be done and what they're willing
to do—this is the breeding ground of fundamental shifts in
society.*

—MICHAEL VENTURA

WHEN EXILES FROM THE WORKPLACE first come to see
me, they arrive in various stages of psychological fragmentation, grief, disbelief, agony, and victimization. The glue that
has held their selves together has dried up to varying degrees,
and they find themselves often without words to describe their
experience. Theirs is often a language of tears, or of repetitious
statements (e.g., "Nobody cares!"), or physical symptoms. For
them, there is no context of meaning in a society where work is
simultaneously the center of existence, and then suddenly no
more than just a job, when one is betrayed and bereft. They
peer at me from their abyss and seek something, often not
knowing what. I see my job simply: to give them words.

Words are placeholders. They locate us. They are terra
firma when we lose our footing, our anchoring, our emotional
homes. They give shape to formless, overpowering affects.
Most important, they bring us into contact with others, into hu-

man community where we are more than a compendium of
physical pains and disruptions, more than tears or rage or
numbness. Words are a beginning. And, with any new beginning, there is hope.

What is missing so often in our understanding of Americans' obsession with their jobs is a language that can capture
people's actual experience. If we are told that the reasons we invest so much of ourselves in work each day are purely rational—that is, to make more money; to build our resumes; to
promote the brand called Us—then all of those emotional
needs so many of us bring to work remain unlabelled, without
words. When we are without words, we are without self-
knowledge and self-understanding. We bake cookies for our
coworkers without fully knowing why. We wear our company's logo on our clothes without forethought. We stay at
work until 10:00 P.M., polishing a report that is supposed to be a
first draft, not thinking of what drives us. We worry about
what our supervisor meant when he ignored us in the hall,
without pausing to ask why it means so much to us. We lack
the words that would allow us to acknowledge what we are
yearning for, what selfobject needs are clamoring for attention
and fulfillment. Without self-understanding we open ourselves
to becoming functions of our employers. Our needs for recognition, acceptance, identity, and security silently mesh with our
employers' needs for a motivated, thoroughly committed
workforce.

The language of being married to the job may not fully
capture people's experience of turning to the workplace for the
satisfaction of unmet emotional needs, but I think it telegraphs
a way of labeling a common experience, which allows a context
of meaning to develop. *Marriage* implies intense emotional

commitment, fidelity, exclusivity, security, reciprocity, personal identity, social acceptance, and access to care and support. When we connect these states of being to the job, we allow for a language that introduces people's psychological lives into the workplace. In so doing we form an infrastructure for self-understanding. We begin to examine our motivations for investing in our jobs.

This chapter will attempt to help individuals put words to the problem that for many has had no name. We will examine how employees can recognize if they are married to their jobs, and what they can do when a workplace divorce looms.

Are You Married to Your Job?

I am often asked how one can recognize whether one is too emotionally involved with one's workplace. I respond by suggesting that one should imagine quitting one's current job and allowing oneself to fully experience what that would feel like. Would you feel: Relieved? Triumphant? Freed? Hopeful? Guilty? Bereft? Alone? Terrified? Without a purpose? Without an identity? Certainly, if any one of the latter sets of feelings emerges, it is reasonable to question one's emotional investment in work.

To get a better sense of whether you are married to your job, take the self-administered test in the Appendix.

In general, it is important to say in words—either out loud or in writing—what it is that attaches one to the workplace. Is it the work itself or is it the praise and recognition that the work can elicit? Or is it primarily the sense of being part of a respected, high-profile, or successful corporation? Does the workplace provide human connection that is absent in the rest of one's life? Ultimately, if we prefer to be at work rather than away from work, chances are we have entered into some form of marital covenant.

Joan, a longstanding member of one of my psychotherapy groups, who had been the Director of Human Resources for a large manufacturing company, recalls that she

> Can remember the day that it hit me. I was standing on a mezzanine [at work] looking out over the floor, and I thought "you know, I care more about this place than my own home." My own home. And I've lived in my house for eighteen years. At that point it really filled me with pride. I think tears came to my eyes. This was *my* company. And I felt kind of choked up inside.

> *Had you ever felt that way before?*
> "Yeah, when my kids were born."

At that point, I think it would have helped Joan enormously to put into words what was so moving to her, what filled her with pride, and why she cared more about her workplace than her home. Her personal identification with her employer, the sense that this was *her* company clearly was filling some unarticulated emotional needs, needs that remained outside of Joan's conscious awareness. Thus, when she was laid off, Joan not only lost her job but her identity and her preferred "home."

Luba states, "I never questioned, never asked myself why I couldn't pull myself away from work. Why I had to rush home to turn on my computer and check my e-mail (from work). I think if someone had said to me: 'Luba, what are you doing? What are you running away from?' maybe I would have been forced to see what I couldn't see." I take this to mean that if she had been compelled to articulate in words what she was acting out behaviorally, she might have been able to *see,* to have self-knowledge. Instead, she lived to work until March 6, 1998, when she was suddenly transferred to another work group. It was only after she left work on disability, and was forced to talk in group therapy about the motivations for marrying her job, that Luba acquired vision.

When I gave my test that appears in the Appendix to one of my groups as a sort of pilot study, Marion shouted out "Bingo! That's me. I really thought I was lucky to have that job." Having overcome such deprivation and adversity in her life, Marion thought she was the luckiest person alive when she was invited into the Phaeton family. I asked if she had ever shared her sense of being so lucky with others, and she replied:

No way. I was sick of being a "success story." I told myself this was just a job, no big deal. But inside I never got used to it. I always secretly thought "this is way too good to be true." But no one ever knew that. Hell, I don't think I really let on *to me* that deep down inside I don't think I deserved it.

Perhaps if Marion had been able to put into words her sense of unworthiness, then her idealization of both Phaeton and her supervisor, Bill, could have been acknowledged and explored. The pervasive sense that she was undeserving of her position as account manager made her enormously vulnerable to Bill's evaluation. Thus, his questioning of her work tapped into Marion's core fear that she was unworthy, a fear that drove her but that remained unspoken and unacknowledged.

Putting words to what one feels, understanding what moti-

vates us, and moving toward self-understanding are the vehi-
cles for recognizing if we are living to work or working to live.
In order to engage in this process, we must have a space—both
in time and in place—for self-reflection. We need unhurried
time for quietly looking within and being curious. It is only
with time that is not instrumentally measured—some might
call it *leisure*—that we can grasp a sense of an interior life, an
inner depth, an identity or selfhood, that stands apart from
what we do.

An expanding work week, electronic leashes, and a work-
obsessed culture that envelops us, stand in opposition to time
for self-reflection. Without a space for connecting our actions,
thoughts, and feelings, for knowing ourselves, we more closely
resemble things, cogs in a machine—means, rather than ends
in our own right. We allow the workplace to dominate us, simply because *us* remains flattened, without depth. Thus, in order
to recapture our sense of identity, we need to push back against
the encroachment on our time, and create a space to know ourselves, in part through establishing emotional and temporal
boundaries at the workplace.

Simple ways of beginning this process can include the following:

- Set clear boundaries. Whenever you are asked to work late,
  work more, or work outside your job description, think
  through the possible ramifications. Why would you say yes?
  What would happen if you say no?
- Try to leave work at a specific time each day. The more time
  we spend at work, the less time and energy we have to
  expend for family, friends, and activities that might provide
  us with self-esteem and a sense of who we are apart from our

jobs. Some of my patients specifically schedule psychotherapy appointments in the late afternoon, so that they are compelled to leave work and have time reserved for themselves.

- Each work day set aside a period of time—at least ten minutes—to reflect on your actions, thoughts, and feelings. Be curious about your motivations, reactions, and desires. Stand apart from what is going on around you, and look at your life from the outside, from the perspective of an *observing ego,* as psychotherapists call it. Go to a park at lunch; sit in your car before entering work in the morning; close your office door; put your head down on your desk during a break; take a walk around the block sometime during the workday; write in a journal while commuting on the train.

- Establish limits on electronic leashes. If you're not on call for your work, make sure you're not checking e-mail and voice mail after hours. If you find yourself drawn to checking in with work in your free time, ask yourself if there is something missing in your personal life. If you're feeling lonely or bored when not electronically connected to the workplace, begin to question what is lacking in your personal life that compels you to be electronically connected to your job.

- If you feel an inner compulsion to run errands, bring muffins, plan parties, and so on, take time to consider what is motivating you. Are you missing social activities or caring for others outside the job? Are you feeling unappreciated and unrecognized for these activities outside the job?

- Try to set aside time each day to get away from the work site. Using your lunch hour to separate yourself from what's going on at work is invaluable for creating an emotional boundary, and engaging in or just thinking about activities that are not work related.

- Make sure that your closest friends are not coworkers. We all need sources of connection and support outside work. If something bad or hurtful happens on the job, it is critical to have people we can turn to, discuss the issues with, and get support from. Turning to colleagues often can lead to more difficulties on the job. In hierarchical work situations where people are vying for attention, praise, and promotions, friendships can easily sour.

- When choosing between attending an activity involving family or friends (e.g., a child's soccer game, a friend's party) and work, ask yourself why you're choosing work. Is it absolutely crucial that you make this choice? If it is, then perhaps it's time to reevaluate this particular job or your own need to invest in the workplace over family and friends.

- Take vacations! Increasingly, Americans are not taking advantage of the relatively meager amount of paid vacation time allotted to them. Even if we don't travel, it is important to take time off to replenish who we are, and to invest in activities that bring us pleasure.

- If you are feeling upset about something that is happening at work, put it into words. E-mail a friend or family member. Write down in a journal what you are feeling, why you think you are feeling this way, and list alternatives of how you might respond. Talk about the problem to family or friends after work. See a therapist. But do not ignore, deny, or dismiss what you are feeling.

What happens if you do end up marrying your job? How can you disentangle yourself, recover from a betrayal, and/or move on after a workplace divorce?

TALKING TO CHANGE

If change occurs it happens on the ground, between persons speaking out of inner need, rather than through mass uprisings.

— RICHARD SENNETT

Recognizing that you are married to your job or suffering a crisis at work can provide an opportunity for tremendous personal change and growth. Psychological transformation can occur when normal defenses are lowered and affect is heightened, when there is a willingness to examine how you have been living your life. To acknowledge that normal ways of coping no longer work can promote self-scrutiny, curiosity about your motivations, and openness to doing things differently, to changing dysfunctional patterns.

Psychotherapy provides a model for individual change. It offers the prospect of hope, transformation, and the reexamination of lifelong assumptions. At its best, it is

the provision of the possibility of a genuine, reliable, understanding, and respecting, caring personal relationship in which a human being whose true self has been crushed . . . can begin at last to feel his own true feelings, and think his own spontaneous thoughts, and find himself to be real. . . .

Seen from a somewhat different perspective, author Vince Bielski argues that psychotherapy is

one of the few sanctuaries left in America where people can recover a more authentic sense of themselves, challenge the mass culture that invades their lives, test in the presence of a sympathetic listener the possibilities for living in ways running against the popular grain and more in tune with what they really want. To the extent that therapy wakens people to alternative ways of thinking and being, helps them find the strength to resist the meretricious and often quite vicious market pressures that define their existence, it has the potential for becoming a quietly revolutionary counterculture with real power to transform society.

For our purposes, Bielski's optimistic view of psychotherapy rests on a therapist's own resistance to *market pressures,* his or her capacity to withstand the pull to overvalue work at the expense of life that exists outside of market transactions. As we have seen from the experience of my patients described in chapter 3, psychotherapy can act to reinforce an individual's sense of self blame or overinvestment in one's workplace, if a therapist does not stand apart from prevailing norms and unquestioned cultural assumptions him- or herself.

Given this crucial proviso, however, at its best, psychotherapy can provide a form of sanctuary, or as Kenneth Gergen has termed it, "time off the merry-go-round" of our work-obsessed, market-drenched lives. It can offer a countervailing perspective, a space from which to evaluate one's life. It is within such space that forgotten dreams, unsatisfied desires, and submerged hopes can be recuperated.

By definition, open-ended, exploratory psychotherapy opposes the emotional asceticism that increasingly characterizes our lives. It asks the patient to identify emotional needs rather than deny them. It calls into question what we do without, what we put up with in our everyday lives, and, in so doing, can stir up pain and dissatisfaction, the prerequisites of change. Its very format of sustained, empathic attention can highlight the hunger so many of us experience for more acknowledgment, recognition, and care in the rest of our lives. And, in so far as it compels us to stop, reflect, see, and take stock, it contains the capacity to transform.

Such transformation can be fundamentally life altering or incremental; it can take months or years, and it is often surprising to both therapist and patient how change does or doesn't proceed. Clearly, I was surprised by Michelle's sudden and complete marriage to her new Silicon Valley job. I think I did not fully recognize both the depth of her need and what I now see as the superficiality of *our* connection. My sense is that Michelle complied, went along with me in my focus on her eagerness to please, her feelings of inadequacy, and the ultimate impossibility of getting her needs met through her workplace, but I don't think she ever fully took these ideas in. She accommodated herself to what she perceived as my world view. In this sense, she was repeating an old pattern of attempting to please an authority figure. At the same time, however, I don't think Michelle ever idealized me in quite the way she did Glenn or Shelby. Perhaps what I was offering her was simply too small and inadequate: one hour of psychotherapy a week and the recommendation to find pursuit outside work that might give her a sense of herself, a feeling of accomplishment, and an opportunity to make real friends. I think this was asking too much, and offered too little support. The enveloping culture of her new job conveyed to her that she didn't need to struggle, change, or even acknowledge the feelings of pain and inadequacy within. Without effort she was home free, and she wanted to believe it. I was asking her for transformation. Her new employer was implicitly telling her to remain the same and she would be rewarded. Her eagerness to please, to sacrifice for others with the hope of being accepted and loved, neatly fit her employer's need for employees who would work long hours and demonstrate fervent commitment to their jobs. Michelle's selfobject needs and her company's mission colluded to drown out my relatively puny voice.

Conversely, Lionel took me by surprise as to how dramatically he turned his life around. After about three months in therapy he told me, "What we've been talking about really got me thinking. I've always believed in VPA as though they were God. But maybe *they're* wrong, you know . . . Maybe I got too caught up in this status thing. None of this would have happened if I stayed put. But they want you to go after the carrot." The carrot was getting a placement in the 60s in VPA's hierarchical levels of occupational importance.

In the months that followed, we began to talk less about what had happened to Lionel at work, and more about recovering and reconnecting with his suppressed dreams. It turns out that, when he was an adolescent, he had aspired to play professional basketball, but his family had dismissed this as a pipe dream. The therapy shifted to focusing on his disappointment and anger at his family, and the lack of recognition and praise he received from his parents. For someone who initially presented himself as having only minimal psychological insight and very little interest in self examination, Lionel has become a true enthusiast for probing his motivations and developing an understanding of his own history. To my surprise, he started reading self-help books; he attended a John Bradshaw workshop on coming to terms with unresolved feelings from childhood; and he has decided to see if he can become a volunteer basketball coach at an after-school program near where he lives. As of this writing, he remains uncertain about how to re-launch his career, but his life is in a state of transformation. However Lionel resolves his dilemma about where to work, he will be unlikely to invest in his job in the same way he did at VPA. Recently he told me that any new job will "have to accept me for who I am. If I've learned anything, it's that I don't have to jump through hoops anymore."

Jim's is a case in which change is more slow and incremental. Jim has used his crisis at work as a vehicle for intense self-scrutiny: Why have others' evaluations of him been the pivot around which he has lived his life? Why has he avoided being alone? What is this feeling of emptiness inside him? Why has he avoided real intimacy with others? Jim continues to work at the same job, but he is trying to examine and question his feelings and actions in the workplace. He has set up boundaries that he never thought of maintaining before. He never works later than 6:00 P.M., at which time he turns off his cell phone and pager. He makes a point of going to the gym for at least one-half hour dur-ing each work day. If he begins to feel overwhelmed by the lack of privacy in his work setting, he leaves the office and goes for a walk. His relationship with the agency's president is a subject that he repeatedly returns to in therapy. He has acknowledged how the most subtle gesture or change in his boss's mood can af-fect not only Jim's own feelings, but his very sense of himself and his self-worth. In this way, he effectively uses psychotherapy as a space for self-reflection and an expanding self-knowledge. I can-not predict if he will continue on at the same job or end up changing either his place of work or his entire career path. Whatever he ultimately decides, his choice will be made from a position of self-understanding he never before possessed.

Luba's use of psychotherapy has been surprising in a way in which I could not have imagined. Luba met with me in once-per-week, individual psychotherapy for a year. Each session had a repetitive, rotelike quality. She rehearsed the same material with the same affect. Every session contained reference to that "terrible date, March 6, 1998," when she was transferred to another work group. Over the course of the year, I learned about Luba's family of origin, her life in the Eastern European town in which she spent her childhood before going to the university, and her travails in attempting to emigrate. All this was background, told to me with little affect or interest. What held Luba's attention and ensnared her mind and her heart was the betrayal she felt she had experienced at work. The repetitious retelling of this betrayal became her mantra, and helped maintain the plethora of physical symptoms that prevented her from returning to any kind of paid employment and which continued to worry her primary-care physician.

Because Luba was making so little headway, I began thinking again of referring her to one of my psychotherapy groups. When I initially made this recommendation within the first month of meeting with her, Luba had asked me what kind of women were in the group. When I told her that most of them held pink collar, that is, clerical or administrative jobs, she responded by informing me that "these are the kind of people who assist me," and that she couldn't imagine sharing what had happened to her at work "with those kinds of people." Because Luba was in so much distress and seemed to have such a need to talk about the trauma that had befallen her, I did not push her, and told myself that individual psychotherapy would meet her needs. I now question my judgment in this matter.

When I again brought up the possibility of her attending

one of my groups after a year of our meeting individually, I acknowledged my sense that Luba was not improving and that I was concerned about her ongoing physical problems, particularly the headaches, shortness of breath, and the numbness and tingling in her hands that had been found to have no physiological etiology. I was surprised that Luba did not feel judged by this observation and that she agreed to come to a group session to see if she fit in.

The group that Luba attended was composed primarily of African-American women, including Grace, Leatrice, and Marion. Teri was also in the group. They tended to be loud, brash, funny, and self mocking. Marion often greeted new members by exclaiming "Welcome to the nut club!" Leatrice liked to crack jokes and would say that the most useful thing about coming to group was that it was the only place in her life that she laughed, "and if I can laugh, I know I'm still me." None of them had been in supervisory positions; they all *were* supervised and often discussed this mutual experience. For all these reasons, I was anxious about Luba coming to the group. I was worried that she would not fit in, that she would be offended, and feel like an outcast, without access to help. I was concerned that in response to such feelings she would be condescending or perhaps even racist. It felt to me that both Luba and I were taking a chance.

At Luba's first group meeting, Grace was discussing her adult daughter's disappointment with her for continuing not to work. This daughter, who worked for the Navy, was complaining that Grace had instilled in her a strong work ethic, and she now felt that her mother wasn't "practicing what she preached." Grace felt profoundly misunderstood but also guilty that "maybe my daughter's right. Maybe I'm letting her

down." At which point Luba, who had not yet spoken, inter-
jected in a forceful voice, "No, you're not letting her down;
she's letting *you* down by not understanding what you're going
through." We all turned to Luba with some degree of surprise.
Then, Leatrice said, "Look Grace, your daughter's probably
scared. She's seen you as this rock all these years and now *you*
have problems, and it's like 'my mamma ain't supposed to be
hurtin'; she gotta be strong' kinda thing." To which Luba
replied, "I think that's right. We all want our parents to be pil-
lars of strength, particularly our mothers." And, with that,
Luba became a member of the group.

Over the next few weeks, Luba's participation in group as-
tonished and intrigued me. She was animated, warm, caring,
outgoing, and truly engaged in the other women's problems.
She laughed at the jokes and seemed utterly without judgment
when Marion referred to her former crack addiction and Teri
showed us her latest body piercing (at which point Grace told
Teri that she "was acting against God's will"). I began to realize
that this exuberant, giving, and accepting Luba was the woman
who had developed the deep connection with her East Indian
coworkers. She thrived in community; she felt she belonged.

After Luba had been in group for about two months,
Leatrice led off a discussion of how emotionally unsupportive
her boyfriend had been since she left her job. Many of the
women chimed in with stories about how the men in their lives
just didn't get it, couldn't comprehend how the workplace
could take such an enormous psychological toll on them. Suddenly, Luba burst forth: "Oh, I know what you mean. My husband couldn't understand if his life depended on it. Everything
is so rational, so orderly, and I disturb the order in his life."

In a year of individual psychotherapy I had never heard

Luba criticize her husband. In fact, I had rarely heard her speak of him, and had suggested to her that it was odd that he seemed to play such an insignificant part in her psychic life. So I intervened and asked Luba what she meant.

"He is cold. He has never understood me. Sometimes, I think he would be happier if he didn't have to deal with me at all."

Grace then asked, "Why do you stay with him then? Why not just up and leave?"

"Believe me I would like to but, in our families, no one divorces. And I have to think about my children, what would happen to them if we divorced."

There ensued a long conversation about the pros and cons of divorce, its effects on children, men's capacity (or lack thereof) for emotional succor, and how a mother should weigh her needs against those of her family. After the group ended, I went out to lunch. When I returned, one hour later, Luba, Grace, and two other women from group were engrossed in an animated conversation on the steps outside my building.

In the group sessions that followed, Luba seemed even more relaxed and happy. She appeared to be giving more attention to how she dressed and wore her hair. She laughed readily, something I had never heard her do in our individual sessions. She was an active participant in all of the discussions, gave helpful comments, shared her own experience, and often left chatting away with the other women as they walked down the hall to the elevator.

One day, a new group member was talking with a great deal of distress about numbness and tingling in her hands that she was experiencing in response to a betrayal at work. I asked Luba if she was still having that symptom and was surprised by her response: "Oh, God, no. I haven't felt that in ages. In fact, I haven't had any problems now for months." Given that Luba's continual and varied physical symptoms of stress had been a focus of our individual therapy sessions, I was amazed not only at their disappearance but at the nonchalance Luba evinced in regard to that disappearance.

"How did your problems go away?" I asked.

"I don't know. They just did," she replied.

So, without any incisive interpretation on my part, without incorporating relaxation techniques or pain management or exercise into her daily routine, and seemingly without a whole lot of acquired insight into her betrayal at work, Luba was recovering and changing. There was simply no question in my mind as to why this was happening. Somehow, group therapy unlocked something inside her, and was allowing a suppressed, buried way of being to emerge. As this process unfolded, Luba found herself acknowledged, accepted, and respected. In many ways, then, Luba's experience exemplifies the power of shared speech, mutual recognition, and breaking the taboo on the silent acceptance of individual failure, that group therapy can provide.

THE IMPORTANCE OF GROUPS

I have come to believe that group psychotherapy is the most effective and powerful means of coping with, and recovering from, a betrayal at work. Whether the betrayal is the result of being fired or laid off, deceived or misled by a supervisor, or simply from recognizing that the workplace is not a family or community, participation in a group can ameliorate the blow, normalize feelings, create a context in which to understand what has happened, and form a countervailing experience from which to view the role of work. I have found that the group process operates on a number of levels that help people understand, recover, and, sometimes, even thrive.

Fundamentally, group therapy allows for a narrative to be constructed. When patients first arrive in group they are frequently at a loss to make sense of what has happened to them. They lack a vocabulary and a context of meaning. They feel awash in symptoms of anxiety, depression, and/or physical distress. Without words, their misery has no containment. They often have experienced the incredulity of friends, family, and, as we saw in chapter 3, professionals to whom they turn for help. They feel alone, exiled, crazy. Then, they arrive and listen as each woman tells a brief version of her story: what happened to her at work, how she came to group, and what has happened to her since then. Each of the stories has a narrative flow, and each contains elements with which the new member can identify. Suddenly, surprisingly, the overwhelming, poorly defined experience has a home and a context. And that sudden sense of home can be enormously powerful. Often, when a new member speaks, she reveals how startled she is to have her story contextualized: "Until now, I thought I was the only one who felt this way," or "I didn't know people could forget where they put their keys (or "could think they were having a heart attack," or "want to give up living," or "not want to get out of the house") because of what happened at work." Brenda, who remained in group therapy for three-and-a-half years, would often tell new members:

> When I'd meet with Ilene, she'd tell me that what I was feeling made sense and that it takes a while to get over something

like this. But inside of me I'd still think "I'm really crazy, and she's just being nice." So when she started the group I was so amazed because we all felt the same way; we all thought we were crazy. . . . I thought I was the only one who felt like I couldn't go out of the house because people would think there was something wrong with me. But then, I come to find out that lots of us feel that way. And so that helped.

Simply hearing the word *betrayal* can telegraph meaning and serve to calm, soothe, and help translate overwhelming feelings into thoughts and words. After Leatrice first told her story to the group with tears running down her face, choking on her anger, Marion exclaimed "Honey, it sounds like you've been betrayed like all the rest of us." To which Leatrice seemed to light up. "Yeah, I have," she quietly responded, and she then sat silently for a minute or two nodding her head. Marion's acknowledgment and empathic understanding of Leatrice's feelings had a salutary effect. The next time Leatrice spoke, she seemed depressed but composed, more thoughtful, more in control of her emotions.

Through feeling that one's experience is understood and, hence, understandable, the core sense of being utterly alone with one's anguish, torment, or terror begins to shift. The bleak landscape of personal failure and despair suddenly appears to have some rays of light peek through. The idea emerges that "maybe I'm not crazy for feeling this way if others feel this way too." This may be the key to group therapy's transformative power. It diminishes shame. The shame of having been vulnerable, having cared so much, invested so much in a job. The shame of wanting acceptance, approval, and praise from others that can make us feel weak, dependent, naïve, incomplete, and/or silly. In our society, in which all of us are expected to be consistently autonomous and self reliant in all aspects of our lives—particularly in our professional roles—to need and to have that need exposed is shameful.

I think, then, that the salient affect in betrayal is shame. For many who feel betrayed at work, shame is quite palpable. When Lionel's new supervisor sarcastically asked him for a report he didn't have, when Brenda's favorite attorney gave theatre tickets she coveted to another secretary, and when Jim's boss criticized him in front of all the other employees, shame was at the very surface of the experience. For others, shame remains more hidden and, perhaps, more global. I think that what underlay Grace's, Sarah's, Marion's, Leatrice's, Bea's, Teri's, and Lin's workplace crises was a feeling of humiliation for caring so much in the absence of reciprocation. It is at the moment when they realize their employer, supervisor, or coworkers don't care in the same way they do, that they feel shamed, deflated, and rejected.

According to psychoanalyst Andrew Morrison, when the "anticipated or hoped for response is not forthcoming, we experience abrupt confusion and deflation, recoiling inward and pulling back, withdrawing from the offending selfobject environment." Thus, when Grace's supervisor, Tanya, demonstrated that she cared more about staffing needs than about Grace's health; when Sarah's boss responded to her request for relief with "If you can't stand the heat, get out of the kitchen"; and when Teri realized that her coworkers didn't want to come to work on New Year's Eve; each felt shamed in the absence of the anticipated or hoped for response.

Shame implies a rejection of the whole self and, in this sense, is more sweeping and absolute than guilt. With the latter, we feel bad about what we have done or have thought about doing. With shame we feel bad for who we *are*. Thus, when patients first come to group, they do not feel that others are mad at them or disappointed in them, or that they haven't lived up to their own expectations, as they might feel if they suffered primarily from guilt. Rather, they feel as though there is something fundamentally wrong with them. They are pathetic, crazy, defective, unlikable, unworthy, weak, disgusting. Given that shame is a relatively wordless state, there is no language to describe the all-encompassing feelings, the sense of total dejection, the misery.

> Like fog, shame distorts vision and influences what is seen. But more. Shame also feels like a weight, a heaviness, a burden, pressing down often at the top of the back, forcing the body into the characteristic posture . . . shoulders hunched, the body curved forward, head down, and eyes averted. . . . Shame induces a wish to become invisible, unseen, to sink into the ground or to disappear. . . .

If one craves invisibility, coming to group therapy can be enormously challenging. Therefore, the very act of attending the first session often allows for a feeling of accomplishment, of mastering a fear. At her first group session, Bea announced: "I'm scared to death to be here and I'm only doing it because Dr. Philipson said I should, but my hands are sweating and I know my pressure's up, and I want to run out. But I know I've gotta try, but God, it's hard."

After Bea told her story, the women in group—all of whom were young enough to be Bea's daughters—were so understanding and welcoming that Bea literally beamed. She had suddenly found a new world of acceptance where she was not made to feel crazy for caring so much about being excluded from lunch by her coworkers. The shame she had felt when her boss, then her family and friends, trivialized her upset, dissipated. And I think Bea—echoing Brenda—explains why this process could not have taken place in individual psychotherapy:

> If it's just another person telling you it's okay, even if that other person is a psychologist, you just don't believe it. You know you figure they're trained to do that. But the day I came into the group and all the girls were nodding and showing me they knew what I was talking about, boy that told me, "Hey, maybe I'm not a basket case."

Given that the shaming experience occurs in a social context—it is in the presence of others that one feels rejected and humiliated—it may take a social context to set one free of feeling ashamed. In many ways, the group provides a corrective selfobject experience. The anticipated, hoped-for response *is* forthcoming. The new member has allowed herself to be seen, her shameful feelings have been revealed, and she is then accepted. A group of one's peers, rather than a lone professional, welcomes, embraces, and understands. All the members have felt some version of shame for investing so much of themselves in their workplaces. Consequently, there is a process of mutual recognition that unleashes one from the sense there is something idiosyncratic and shameful in one's response.

Once the profound sense of shame, and its attendant need for invisibility, begin to dissolve, the new group member can begin to look inside and reflect. The group process enforces the importance of understanding one's motivations. Following my lead, group members ask each other "Why do you think that was so important to you?" "How did that make you feel?" "Why didn't you stand up to him?" "What makes you think you're crazy for feeling that way?" The members and I maintain a culture that opens up people's inner lives, rather than closing them down. At its best, group creates a space for reflection and expansion, a space to realize oneself, a space that values individuals for who they are rather than for what they do. In this sense, group offers a significant counterbalance to the workplace. As writer Vince Bielski notes:

> What emerges most strongly from talking to clinicians who think about the problem of work in their clients' lives is the powerful (if often unrecognized) need people have for sanctuary, a space and time that is both more personal and private than work life, but also broader and more spacious than the confined, cramped and claustrophobic world of The Job.

A frequent question that new members ask is "Why is it taking me so long to get over this?" And my response is always "How do we determine *so long*? How do we know how long healing and recuperation is supposed to take?" The most typical response is "I should just be able to get over it and get back to work." I use this as an example of how we are accustomed to ignoring feelings, to overriding what is going on inside us, in order to work and be productive. Knowing what we feel, examining what we are experiencing, is too frequently seen as a luxury, or a sign of malfunction, an inability to keep up, get with it, face reality, stop bitching, get back on the horse, smell the coffee, get a grip, get a life, get over it. These are exhortations my patients hear from their families and friends, and it is what they tell themselves. Our culture is replete with injunctions about how to treat ourselves instrumentally, how to deny what we feel, how to make ourselves emotional ascetics. Group provides a different way of being with different values. It can challenge not only what one has experienced at work, but also what one may have been exposed to throughout one's life. After being in group therapy a year and a half, Brenda spoke poignantly about this issue. "Coming to group for so long now makes me think about what I haven't had in my life. No one in my family ever seemed to have the time to ask me what I was feeling or if I was sad or anything. I thought that was normal; nothing was wrong with it."

Group can demonstrate how little attention, recognition, and care people have learned to put up with. It can prompt them to see what they have been missing and why they attempt to satisfy emotional needs at work. It can also function to help them see how their attempts at getting their needs met may appear to others. As psychoanalyst Malcolm Pines notes, group therapy

> both enables and requires persons to look at and listen to others, to themselves, and consider, perhaps accept, the viewpoint of others. This is an opportunity to see ourselves "in the round," to see those invisible and hidden dimensions which constitute our individual selves, for just as we cannot see our physical selves without reflections from mirrors, so we cannot perceive ourselves as social persons without the seeing and hearing of the responses of others to us and considering, if not always accepting, the ways in which we are experienced by others.

My muffin-club group proved to be an outstanding example of how members can learn to see their ways of being social persons through the responses and reflections of others. As the group cohered, each member became freer in questioning others' perceptions and behaviors. After Sarah had been in group for a couple of months, it was her turn to check in and tell the group how her week had been. She said, "It looks like Joan really has something to say, so, why doesn't she talk? I can wait until next week." Brenda then wondered aloud if "this is the kind of thing you'd do at work, Sarah? I mean, taking care of others and ignoring what you need?"

Because each member was so attuned to each other's eagerness to please, to search for acceptance and caring through self-sacrificing behavior, the muffin club achieved a remarkable level of openness and honesty. It deeply affected not only its members' stance toward work, but their personal relationships as well. By the time Brenda, then Sarah, left group, each had experienced significant transformation in her life.

Brenda ended up spending almost four years in group. Her feeling that she had been betrayed at the law firm became an entrée into an examination of her history and her present. For the first time in her life, she allowed herself time and space for reflection and, in so doing, she faced up to the tremendous pain she had sequestered within. As the fifth of six children in a working-class family, in which both parents worked long hours and the father was an alcoholic, Brenda learned early on to expect little in the way of time, attention, or much care from her family. In order to not reexperience the pain and neglect she had felt as a child, as an adult, Brenda had little to do with her family of origin. Her marriage had ended in a bitter divorce and, because she spent so much time at work, Brenda had little beyond work to engage or sustain her. She threw herself into work, seeking to fulfill selfobject needs for recognition, for belonging to an idealized group, for a sense of identity, and the caring regard of others. She was, thus, emotionally vulnerable to the attorneys for whom she worked. Like the other muffin-club members, Brenda unconsciously believed that if she pleased her employer through the enactment of familistic, second-shift activities, she would be the star, the favorite. She would not only be accepted into this much admired and idealized family, she at last would be recognized for her special qualities. When this strategy failed, Brenda collapsed, and it took her four years to reconstruct her sense of self.

Brenda eventually became the "star" of group. Her relatively long tenure, combined with her accumulated insight and warm personality, allowed her to become a virtual co-leader of the group with me. As new members arrived, Brenda offered them reassurance, normalized their feelings, and spoke with authority about the process of breakdown, grief, anger, self scrutiny, acceptance and moving on. Her mentoring status gave her a powerful feeling of mastery. On her last day in group, she summarized her experience succinctly:

When I first came here, I felt like killing myself. I loved my job, and it still makes me want to cry when I think of it. . . . The group gave me hope; I couldn't have survived without it. I knew I wasn't alone anymore. I really felt that you became like sisters to me. . . . I feel like I went from being the most crazy one [in the group] to being sort of an inspiration: If Brenda can make it, then anyone can! [laughs]. . . . I'm never going to look to a job for my identity, and I'm never going to let anyone I work for have that kind of power over me. I know it'll be hard, but I know all of you and Ilene will be here rooting for me.

Brenda took a new job working in the science department of a nearby university. At my urging, she looked for interests and activities outside work that might provide her with a sense of belonging, purpose, and friendship. She located these by becoming a member, then an informal leader, of a local ACA group (Adult Children of Alcoholics). She continued in her relationship with her boyfriend, Barry, but without any intention of living together or marrying. She would occasionally, and unexpectedly, show up in group. For the first year after leaving the muffin club, Brenda visited every two to three months to provide us with "progress reports." These visits trailed off, and an entire year went by before her next visit. At this session (the last at which I saw her), Brenda let us know how she was faring:

> I can't say it's been easy. I still miss (the law firm). But I've been good at work. Whenever they ask me to stay late or go the extra mile I think about the group and what everyone would say. . . . ACA's been great, and I can talk about my childhood and all the shit I had to put up with. . . . But you know nothing will ever really compare to all that excitement at work (at the law firm). A day doesn't go by when I don't think about them.

Sarah's path to overcoming her workplace betrayal has been easier than Brenda's, simply because she looked to her employer for the satisfaction of far fewer emotional needs. Sarah used PeoplePoint largely as a replacement community in which she could feel a sense of identity and belonging. She effectively used group and, specifically, the muffin-club version of it, as a transitional community in which to understand herself in the company of like-minded peers. In group, she quickly

gained perspective on the ways in which she sacrificed her interests and needs for those of others, and gained her sense of self from being part of a community. As she acquired insight into her motivations, Sarah found herself desiring something more in life that she couldn't quite identify: "I know I have to put myself first and think about what's best for *me*. But I don't know what that is. I've spent my whole life thinking about everybody else and I know I can't do that anymore, but it's hard when you're not used to it."

Sarah took a year to spend time with her sons and contemplate her future. She scraped by on unemployment and child-support payments. Group served as a community for her, and she developed friendships with many of the women—including Brenda and Bea—that extended to activities and mutual support outside group sessions. Finally, she decided that she wished to finish her college degree, something she had abandoned in order to marry her husband when she was twenty-one. She applied to a local state college in computer science and was accepted. We had a farewell party for Sarah on her last day in group, one week before the start of fall semester. I have not seen or heard from her since then, but Bea keeps me informed about how she is faring.

Bea is the only remaining member of the muffin club. She comes to group faithfully, even though the members have changed over the years. She states clearly that group serves a social function for her, something she yearns for since she is now retired. She keeps in touch with most of the muffin-club members who have moved on. They talk on the phone, occasionally meet for lunch, and once had a reunion in Bea's backyard. Sarah came to that party, which was held shortly after she had accepted a job working for a local hospital, providing technical support in the information technology department. For the reunion, Bea had buttons made for each of the women that showed a muffin with a slash going through it. Bea wears her button to each of the group meetings she now attends and regales the current members with tales of "the muffins" she continues to see and talk with. She is our sage and our historian. She is liked and respected for the sense of continuity and connection she brings to group, qualities for which she felt disdained at her workplace.

What Bea's experience poignantly illustrates is how much so many of us wish to be recognized and accepted by others for what we have to offer, and how meager our opportunities often are to satisfy this wish beyond work. Given the growing trend toward greater and greater degrees of social fragmentation and isolation, for many, group therapy can serve as the only example of participating with others in some sort of joint project that is not related to work. For others, belonging to a volunteer organization, a religious congregation, study group, sports team, or twelve-step program, can serve many of the same functions of group therapy. They demonstrate that one can be accepted and recognized by other people, working in concert toward a goal that is not determined by an employer.

Given that the women in my psychotherapy groups experienced some form of betrayal in a social setting, receiving acceptance and support in a social setting can bring about change. It implicitly conveys that isolation, retreating into the self out of shame, is not necessary. It offers the opportunity to learn the lessons of rupture and repair with others. If there is a disagreement or misunderstanding among members of the group, the aggrieved parties can learn how to work through the problem without retreating into victimization, hopelessness, and defeat. A clear example of this occurred when

Leatrice seemed to condemn Marion for her lasting preoccupation with her supervisor, Bill.

> Leatrice: "Girl, you gotta forget about him. We *know* it was bad, but no man, and certainly no *white* man is worth this."

> Marion: "What do you mean, no *white man*?"

> Leatrice: "I mean you made him the executor of your will."

> Marion: "Yeah, and I thought this was why we're all here. We all did crazy stuff for our jobs."

> Leatrice: "Well there's crazy and then there's crazy."

At which point Marion began to cry and ran out of the room. Grace ran after her. I intervened and asked the group what they thought was going on.

> Teri: "Well I think we all like to think of ourselves as strong women and maybe it's a little hard to hear how much Bill hurt Marion ..."

> Leatrice (cutting off Teri): "It *is* hard ..."

> Teri: "And maybe because Bill was white and Marion gave him so much power over her ..."

> Luba (to Leatrice): "And you're very clear about not having men call the shots."

> Leatrice: "That's right. It's kind of painful to me seeing this beautiful, strong woman—she been through so much in her life—to be taken down like that."

When Marion reentered the room, I asked her to tell us how she felt.

Marion: "I felt judged by Leatrice. I felt she was saying I was crazy for how I acted on my job."

Leatrice: "Okay. I think I misspoke because I'm still angry at what happened to me, what happened to all of us."

Toward the end of the session, Marion told us that she was

proud of myself for coming back. I think before I would have just gone home and closed the curtains and put the pillow over my head and said to myself "See, you can't trust anybody. Everybody thinks I'm nuts." But, you know, I stood up to it. Well thanks to Grace, but thanks to Leatrice too because I know you're hurting and you're mad at what happened to me at Phaeton.

At the end of the session Marion and Leatrice embraced, then started laughing. Each had learned that it was possible to experience an interpersonal rupture, to work it through, and recover. The group experience is not about uncritical support for people who have been similarly hurt and betrayed. Rather, it is about the use of empathic understanding to reach across the spaces that distance us from each other and keep us isolated in our sense of personal failure. It is about the struggle for mutual recognition, interpersonal connection, and the capacity to view each other as subjects. It is about the possibility of working together to change. Thus, it is about the potential to create alternative institutional anchors in our lives that are outside the workplace and the market.

It is too soon to know exactly what will happen to many of the women in group. While both Leatrice and Grace are contemplating disability retirement, Marion is increasingly anxious to return to the workforce. She is even thinking of returning to her job working under Bill. Now that she has acquired a better understanding of her needs and motivations, she feels she may be able to resist the pull to both idealize her supervisor and to obtain her sense of identity through working at Phaeton.

She explains, "So, I've been thinking that with both my girls gone [to college] maybe I need to think about getting me some love in my life. Maybe I've proved that I can do it all, and maybe I need to think 'what will make Marion happy?'"

To this end, Teri has been bringing Marion videotapes she has recorded of *Sex and the City,* thinking that these may lure Marion away from her obsession with *The Godfather* movies. Teri has yet to be successful in this regard, but Marion's willingness to watch what Teri brings in, and then discuss some of the issues they elicit in group, suggests a willingness to explore, to be open to a life that is not centered on work.

Teri herself continues to work at Cassie, as she has throughout her tenure in group. In many ways she has withdrawn emotionally from the child-care center and has made it her mission to treat her work there "as just a job." "I'm there to take care of the kids and that's all." She has explored the idea of changing careers but has decided for now to remain a child-care teacher, as she truly seems to feel happiest when she is caring for her charges, but she has found it extremely difficult to build a life outside the workplace. Everyone in group, including myself, has made suggestions as to what she might become involved in, how she might meet people, but none of these has met with much success.

"It's hard to live down there [in Silicon Valley]," Teri states. "How do you make friends when everyone's at work? People think it's this real exciting place to be and maybe it is if you're, you know, one of those big time players. But it's not like Carly Fiorina [the CEO of Hewlett Packard] is knocking at my door asking me out to play."

Teri is depressed, alone, and turns far too much to food and marijuana to quell her pain. I have recommended a trial of antidepressant medication, but she refuses this suggestion for reasons I find difficult to disagree with. "Am I the problem, or is it this world I'm living in?" she asked when I first raised the issue. It is a question we often come back to, in various guises and with different perspectives.

Psychotherapy, even in its group form, ultimately takes as its subject the individual. It allows words, affects, understanding, and self acceptance to emerge. It makes the unconscious conscious and brings to life the repressed past. And, in so doing, it can allow a patient to see how one's history lives on in one's actions, thoughts, and feelings in the present. It provides hope, new ways of thinking about oneself, and oneself in relationship. It can counter culturally pervasive ways of living and thinking through offering a time and space off the merry-go-round of a life centered on work. It does, however, reach a limit, an obdurate social reality that an individual cannot change, at least not alone. In many ways, I think it is this social reality that Teri is encountering in her attempts to make a life for herself outside work.

"In times like these, the trained therapeutic eye, specifically its tendency to focus on individual psychodynamics or family relational difficulties, can be profoundly myopic unless the gaze is adjusted to include the outside world," writes Vince Bielski. What my experience with my patients has shown me is that psychotherapy can effect recovery and change, but change that leads to what? As Teri's case illustrates, she can recognize how she has turned to work for the satisfaction of unmet needs, then change her stance toward her job. But, what then? What if the world she encounters is fragmented, without places to go and things to do that connect her with others and with a sense of identity, belonging, and purpose? In many ways her geographic community in Silicon Valley represents the apotheosis of life in the new economic order. But this community, this model that societies throughout the world seek to emulate, leaves her with only herself to fall back on, only herself to blame for not being Icon Woman, a Change Insurgent, a Brand Called Me.

Ultimately, then, I have come to believe that there are no purely individual solutions to marrying one's job. There are correctives, strategies, and better and worse ways of managing our lives in the new economy. As my patients' experiences demonstrate, when we create emotional and temporal boundaries at work, we are often left looking out at a social landscape that seems devoid of connection, care, and purpose. If we are compelled to depend less on our workplace for commitment and security, where do we turn to feel anchored, sheltered from the endless change, risk, and uncertainty we are enjoined to embrace? In order to cease living to work, Americans need far more than psychotherapy. Talking to each other is a beginning. However, it is only when that talk starts to question our basic cultural assumptions and values that new ways of seeing ourselves and the world around us can emerge. There may be no clear answers, but we certainly can begin to ask the hard questions, the questions that too few of us seem to be asking today.

CHAPTER SEVEN

Escape from Freedom

IN JULY 2001, I RECEIVED A CALL from a local psychiatric inpatient unit telling me that a patient of mine had been admitted the night before due to a suicide attempt. Lin, the Vietnamese woman who had been laid off from what she called "my company" six months prior, had taken an overdose of sleeping pills and turned on the gas in her condominium. She was found by the building manager after he smelled gas coming from her unit.

After a day of calling and not getting through, I finally reached Lin on the patient phone in the locked unit where patients who are a danger to themselves or others are hospitalized. When I asked her what had happened, she replied in a tone that seemed unchanged from the one I had heard repeatedly in group over the course of the past number of months. Without much affect she simply replied, "I have nothing to live for. I will never be the most valuable employee."

Lin had stopped coming to group on a regular basis. When questioned about this, she explained that she had very limited funds and found the copayment required by her HMO to attend group ($25.00) an amount that was difficult to come up with on a weekly basis. She did attend periodically, repeating the same phrases, expressing the same sense of disbelief, loss, and profound dislocation. More than any patient whom I have seen for a workplace divorce, Lin appeared thoroughly lost and disoriented. Prior to her suicide attempt, she had not been in group for over a month. When I had called her at home to see how she was, she had told me that she was "okay, just a little low on funds." I realize now that this was not the whole reason for her lack of attendance. I clearly did not realize how truly desperate she had become.

When she and I finally met after her discharge from the hospital, she was more subdued than I had ever seen her. We talked about the days she had spent in her condo leading up to the suicide attempt, how she had satfor hour after hour, motionless, without thoughts or feelings, forgetting to eat or shower or feed her cat. At one point, she put on the dress she had worn at the last awards dinner and sat quietly in front of a full-length mirror, contemplating all she had lost. "And that's when I decided to do it, to take my life. No one would know; no one would care. *They* (her employer) wouldn't care. So why not?" She then coaxed her cat out the door and closed it behind him, turned on the gas stove and swallowed every pill she had in the house. She states that she lost consciousness thinking peacefully about the obituary she imagined appearing in the paper following her death: MOST VALUABLE EMPLOYEE FOUND DEAD AFTER LAYOFF.

"Do you wish you had succeeded?" I asked.

"Yes," Lin replied with certainty. And then after a long pause, she said "I do not think you understand, Dr. Philipson. You see, I really don't have anything to live for."

We sat in silence for a long time. And, in a way I had not allowed myself to think before, I took in the history of Lin's life and the reality of what stood before her. Rather than expressing my typical reassurances about remaining hopeful, fighting for oneself, remembering the potential we all have to change, contribute, and find happiness, I allowed Lin's feelings to enter me and weigh upon me. My time-honored comments about being married to one's job, not putting all one's eggs in one basket, needing to develop a life outside of work, seemed unbearably chirpy and superficial.

From the outside, Lin's was a true American success story. Having escaped a life of grinding poverty in Vietnam, Lin came to the United States and found employment, along with both her siblings. As an immigrant with only an eighth-grade education and as a single woman, Lin had found remarkable success. She had purchased her own condominium with a view of the bay. She drove a late-model Camry and bought her clothes at Nordstrom and Saks. She was highly regarded at work and compensated well for what she did. She experienced a degree of freedom, autonomy, and financial reward literally unimaginable in her country of origin and throughout most of the world. Her life story represents the apotheosis of the American dream. And that is precisely why I have come to believe that the phenomenon of being married to a job cannot be seen exclusively in individual terms. If Lin's life can be deemed a success, then, we as a society need to begin to question our understanding of success, our values and priorities—that is, the American dream.

Behind Lin's material possessions and long work hours was a life without depth, connection, or meaning. Despite earning $60,000 per year at the time of her layoff, Lin spent everything she made and then some. She had no savings, and a sizable amount of credit-card debt. Thus, as she approached her seventh month of unemployment, too depressed to search for work, she was unable to make ends meet, anxious about fore-closure, bankruptcy, and the ultimate fear plaguing single women: homelessness.

This lack of a material safety net was duplicated in Lin's absence of any kind of human safety net. Due to her whole-hearted dedication to her job, Lin had lost touch with her family. When Lin was twenty-four, her mother married an American and moved to Tucson. Due to her long hours and her reluctance to take vacation time, Lin had visited her mother only twice in the past fifteen years, and talked to her on the phone less and less as the years went by. She felt that her mother, who was uneducated and did not work, could not understand Lin's life, a life centered in a corporate world about which her mother knew nothing. Lin's two brothers remained in the Bay Area, although in suburban, outlying areas. They both had wives and children. Lin made a point of always inviting this extended family to the company awards dinners. Aside from these events, and obligatory visits to their homes for Christmas and sometimes Thanksgiving, however, Lin had little contact with her brothers, sisters-in-law, nieces, and nephews. Her mother's brother lived in San Francisco, but Lin eschewed contact with him. She felt that he was too much a part of the Vietnamese community, for which she had disdain. To her, the Vietnamese were insufficiently integrated into the work world that Lin idealized. They all "worked in restaurants or nail salons. . . . You just don't see them working in *big* jobs," she told me.

This disdain extended to people outside her family as well. Because she is attractive, Lin was often asked out on dates. She usually found the men she saw to be either insufficiently successful in their jobs or unable to accept Lin's preoccupation with her own work. Potential friends also fell prey to this criticism, so that when Lin was laid off she felt she had no one in her life to turn to for any form of support. When I asked about her mother, brothers, the boyfriend with whom she recently had broken up, and the coworkers with whom she occasionally went out for drinks as possible sources of understanding or help, Lin shot back:

"I don't want them to know."

"Why not?"

"To them I am a success. I don't want them to see me like this."

"And what is 'like this?'"

"A failure. I can't make it on my own."

THE TRIUMPH OF INDIFFERENCE

The structure of modern society affects man in two ways simultaneously: he becomes more independent, self-reliant, and critical, and he becomes more isolated, alone, and afraid.
— ERICH FROMM

Lin's story leading up to her layoff represents an extreme version of what I think we as a society have come to define as our way of life, our understanding of success, happiness, and fulfillment. Lin appeared to be completely self sufficient, dependent on no one. Through hard work alone, she had fully assimilated into the mainstream culture and was materially comfortable, physically attractive, and respected at her job. She worked long hours, embraced company culture, and welcomed change. With each new management directive, Lin did not merely go along, but was a cheerleader. She was enthusiastic and charming. She aspired to own her own home, and met that goal without help from anyone, at the age of thirty-four. All this was accomplished against the background of her humble beginnings in Vietnam.

In truth, Lin's life was a Potemkin village that not only fooled others, but fooled Lin herself. Her extreme desire to fit in coupled with the absence of anything inside of her that would have permitted self reflection, perspective, or the capacity for critical thinking about what she was doing, allowed her to become a function of "my company." Her employer became her universe, and its most valuable employee award her raison d'etre Without education, without recourse to institutional anchors, Lin's life was all surface without depth. Lin had only media symbols of success to emulate. Her constant work, her total independence and seeming material success, that is, her achievement of the American dream, ultimately rendered her isolated, alone, and afraid. A layoff revealed a life without meaning and connection.

Americans have always valued hard work. Historically, that value coexisted with others: sacrifice for family, community, and country; altruistic participation in a democratic civic life; belief in God; and the "familistic" qualities described in chapter 5, that is, commitment, sharing, cooperation, and loyalty. As we have become less tethered to family and community, and more insistent that adulthood, maturity, and responsibility are measured primarily by participation in the paid labor force, work has moved to the center stage of our lives and our commitments. We increasingly look with suspicion and condescension at someone who does not work, far more than we question someone who does not make long-term personal commitments through marriage, living with someone, or having children. We value and admire the adult who spends his or her life living alone, working long hours, more than the individual who cares for others at home. Thus, Lin could pass not only as a high functioning adult, but as someone thoroughly enviable and admirable. That her life ultimately was empty and without connection or meaning did not seem to matter as long as she was married—to her job.

We invest in our long work hours, our hectic schedules, our absence of free time as a reflection of success, as we denigrate long-term commitments, interdependence, and care. As Erich Fromm noted long ago, as we become more unencumbered and autonomous from each other, we become more isolated and insecure. In order to escape the pain of that isolation, we turn to new forms of bondage. Our freedoms from tradition render us too alone and, without fully recognizing what we are doing, we surrender our freedom. When Fromm wrote during the Second World War, he saw fascism as the means by which humanity seemed to be rushing forth to surrender the freedom that seemed to have "become a burden, too heavy for man to bear." Fromm looked at that aspect of freedom:

> the powerlessness and insecurity of the isolated individual in modern society who has become free from all bonds that once gave meaning and security to life. We have seen that the individual cannot bear this isolation; as an isolated being he is utterly helpless in comparison with the world outside and therefore deeply afraid of it; and because of his isolation, the unity of the world has broken down for him and he has lost any point of orientation. He is therefore overcome by doubts concerning himself, the meaning of life, and eventually any principle according to which he can direct his ac-

tions. Both helplessness and doubt paralyze life, and in order to live man tries to escape from freedom. . . . He is driven into new bondage.

Given this framework of thought, I would ask: Has our invest-ment in work over all else become a new form of bondage? In order to survive in our social world with its geography of frag-mentation, isolation, and absence of care, are we turning to the workplace for the security and meaning that our "freedoms" have taken from us? Do we submit ourselves to the authority of the workplace in order to escape the *freedom* of living with-out commitments and obligations to others? I think these are the questions that being married to the job ultimately raise.

As we work more, we rely on each other less. Each of us faces the paid labor force autonomously. If we do not succeed, our life is a failure because, as Lin so aptly states, "I can't make it on my own."

This standard of human worth, that is, making it on one's own regardless of gender, age, or circumstance, is relatively new. Previously, people were embedded in families, communi-ties, or labor unions, supported by the state through welfare and social programs, able to rely on churches, neighbors, or friends in hard times. There were means other than work with which to measure oneself as a human being. There was also simply more recognition for our being interdependent. In the distant past, we relied on each other to build barns, fight fires, and pro-vide for needy neighbors when illness or bad harvests put peo-ple at risk. More recently, there was a greater acceptance of the idea that bonding together as working people could secure shorter hours, higher wages, and better benefits. We believed that the role of government was to protect and assist its citizens through hard times. Certainly, the division of labor at home cemented women's dependence on men's wages, and also men's and women's reliance on each other. This has all changed, both in practice and in belief. We deny our interdependence and conflate it with weakness. To be in need is to be needy. To be unencumbered is to be free. And to be free allows one to work excessively long hours. New economy employers play on this perverse sense of freedom through their preference for the *zero-drag* employee. In determining the best employees to hire, many employers calculate prospective hires' *drag coefficient*:

0 = best

1 point for a girlfriend or boyfriend

1 point for each 10 miles of commute to work

1 point for sick parents

1 point for each child

2 points for a spouse

Work and relationships, work and personal commitments, work and caretaking, now more than ever are at loggerheads for all social classes.

As a society, our devotion to work and our veneration of the market have brought indifference into the very core of our social fabric. Market transactions, by definition, are founded in indifference, and indifference is the opposite of love, connection, and care. It, more so than hate which implies an emotional tie, renders us alone and insignificant. As we spend more of our time and energies at work and as more of life outside of work is brought into the market, we become a society that is remarkably uncaring and indifferent. We have freed ourselves from the tyranny of obligatory bonds, long-term commitments,

and the authority of families and communities to supervise and constrain us. The fact that the labor force now welcomes men and women alike theoretically gives all of us the opportunity to be self-supporting, autonomous individuals. However, all of this freedom *from* seems to have rendered many of us insecure, and unsure of what is meaningful and right. Freedom can only exist in a context of security. And without feeling secure, institutionally anchored, connected, and attended to, we seem all too ready to shackle ourselves to the workplace.

To whom do I matter? is a question that is at the heart of my patients' experience. Having believed that they mattered to their employers, they are forced by what they see as a workplace betrayal to confront the fact of indifference, of mattering to few or none. According to Richard Sennett:

> Who needs me? is a question of character which suffers a radical challenge in modern capitalism. The system radiates indifference. It does so in terms of the outcomes of human striving, as in winner-take-all markets, where there is little connection between risk and reward. It radiates indifference in the organization of absence of trust, where there is no reason to be needed. And it does so through reengineering of institutions in which people are treated as disposable. Such practices obviously and brutally diminish the sense of mattering as a person, of being necessary to others.

Being necessary to others, mattering to others, and, thus, affirming our humanity, seems to have less resonance today for so many of us. The ethic of the new economy is founded in openness to change, risk, and uncertainty. One person matters only in so far as he or she performs a task, and is then willing to exit the

scene without complaint. Increasingly, however, this expectation is not limited to the workplace, but permeates our personal relationships where growth, moving on, getting on with one's life, letting go, eschewing "codependence," and following one's own self interest are the hallmarks of maturity. As the logic of indifference suffuses more of our market-driven lives, we overlook our needs to matter to, depend on, and care for others.

If we cannot approach the paid labor force as independent actors, if we suffer from panic attacks or carpal-tunnel syndrome that make it difficult to work, or we can't find child care we can afford, or we need to take care of a sick child or parent, we face an indifferent landscape. What all my patients reiterate is that they cannot turn to others for help because "everyone works" or "they have their own lives." Few belong to labor unions, or religious or fraternal organizations that can assist. And certainly, the state no longer provides a safety net that might foster that most dreaded of human conditions—dependence. When Rush Limbaugh suggested in 1992 that America replace the eagle as our national symbol with a "huge sow that has a lot of nipples and a bunch of fat little piglets hanging on them, all trying to suckle as much nourishment from them as possible," he represented an extreme version of our national outlook: to admit any kind of dependence is ultimately infantile and pathetic.

I would argue, however, that the more we reject our mutual dependence in order to face the market as thoroughly independent actors, the more we learn to feel ashamed in regard to our needs to be cared for, attended to, and helped out. We can react to this shame by hiding, literally, as many of my patients do, within their own homes. Or we can pretend that these needs don't matter through devoting ourselves to work and/or consumption. If we focus our attention on our next purchase, we can

pretend that not feeling cared for or valued is immaterial if we can drive around in an SUV or wear designer clothes. Or we can go on the offensive—much like Rush Limbaugh—and assert that any kind of dependence is pathological, a sign of weakness.

All these strategies, however, allow the problem to fester, preserving our interior sense of shame over wanting security, or care, or the need to matter to others. Without permission to admit our dependency needs, we are left with the shame of not measuring up, of not making it on our own, of not feeling comfortable with all our freedoms to work tirelessly, consume endlessly, and live autonomously.

When the recognition of our mutual dependence is relegated to the shadows of our psychic life and our social landscape, we are diminished as individuals and as a society. When we no longer feel we can rely on each other directly, I would argue that we are more likely to feel alone, depressed, and insecure, and more vulnerable to attaching ourselves to the workplace as a strategy to matter, feel cared for, recognized, and connected. When that strategy fails—as it has for most of my patients—there is nothing emotionally or socially to fall back on. "The social bond arises most elementally from a sense of mutual dependence," writes Richard Sennett. "[S]hame about dependence has a practical consequence. It erodes mutual trust and commitment, and the lack of these social bonds threatens the working of any collective enterprise."

A Leftover Dream

The long-held promise that technology and increased productivity would one day deliver the four-hour work day or the three-day work week, giving us all more leisure time to enjoy our children, write poetry, raise flowers and form

*amateur opera companies now sounds like the sappiest
leftover bubble-dream of a more innocent era.*

—Vince Bielski

Growing up in America after the Second World War, I believed that scientific and technological progress would not only
make our lives easier (we would resemble the Jetsons and live
in Tomorrowland-like environments), but we would work
less. The march of progress would increasingly free us all from
the burdens of work. This placing in opposition to each other,
work and freedom, necessity and liberation, was elaborated for
me by the counterculture that enveloped me when I entered
college in 1969.* I was part of a social movement that eschewed
paid labor, *alienated* labor, and embraced leisure. Hanging out,
that is, unstructured time, time to spend with friends, time to
reflect, wonder, and muse, was an overriding goal. Creative
work—baking bread, gardening, engaging in traditional
forms of art like painting or playing music—and working to
realize social change, to make a difference in the world, were
highly valued. Working in salaried positions that had no other
ends than making money and acquiring status was not. We, of
course, were college students largely from middle- and upper-
middle-class families who had the freedom to imagine such a
future. That is, we were precisely that class of people that now
works more hours than those Americans further down in the
class hierarchy.‡

---

*Of course, this was not a position unique to the 1960s. In 1930, the British
economist John Maynard Keynes predicted that by 2030 economic advances would allow the English to choose to work fifteen hours per week.

‡As Robert Reich points out: "The richer you are, the more likely it is that
you are putting in long and harried hours at work, even obsessing about it

That sense of valuing leisure and creative or altruistic work gradually began to diminish, as my generation grew up and the post–World War II economic boom began to bust. Somewhere in the background of my awareness I realized I was seeing friends less, working more, relaxing less, and talking about work more. However, at some point in the early 1990s, this awareness was sharply brought to the foreground for me. It happened on a Sunday morning in a study group.

For some four or five years, I had been meeting with a group of psychologists and psychiatrists on a monthly basis to discuss topics and readings having to do with psychology and social issues. All of us had been part of the New Left and the counterculture in some form or another, so that we all had shared values that held getting ahead, consuming, and getting rich in some contempt. We had developed a custom of scheduling our next meeting at the end of each study group. On this particular Sunday, each of us got out his or her date book and looked for a time to meet the following month. For some reason, we couldn't find a time. Everybody was overscheduled. There were professional meetings, seminars, editorial board meetings, conferences, papers to be written, talks to be delivered, patients to be seen, work retreats, and classes. Each time someone would propose a date, another member would say "I can't, I have to give a paper in Boston that weekend," or some such thing. This went on and on as we looked over our schedules for the next two months.

This experience was startling on a number of counts. First,

---

when you're not doing it. A frenzied work life may or may not make you better off, but being better off definitely seems to carry with it more frenzy." (*The Future of Success,* op cit., p. 5).

we had never faced such difficulty in years of meeting together. Second, I perceived that my fellow study-group members were not alarmed about this erosion of their free time.
Quite frankly, not only were they not alarmed, they seemed be
proud of their overburdened schedules. Suddenly we seemed
to be engaged in oneupmanship. They did not appear to be
unhappy about not finding a time to meet as they announced
their upcoming commitments. Perhaps my reaction was col-
ored by own situation. As I sat there looking at my date book,
examining each of the proposed dates that met with someone
announcing "No, I can't do it then because I have to . . . ," I
had a sickening realization: *I could meet on each of the dates
proposed.* That is, I was free, without any weekend professional commitments, for the next two months. And this was
what was most startling of all: I was *mortified* by this realization. I felt ashamed. All at once, I experienced myself as unsuccessful, lesser than. Because I had arranged my life in such
a way that I had free time, I was a loser. So, I fell quiet, silently
deciding not to reveal my inadequacies and vowing to change
my life, that is, to become overburdened, time deprived, married to my job, just like my colleagues.

For a time, I succeeded in my ambition. I had a forty-hour
per week, staff psychologist job, and a private practice seeing
patients an additional ten to fifteen hours a week. I began an advanced clinical-training program that met on weekends. I complained about how overtaxed I was, how little free time I had. I
was cool. I had status. Eventually, I could add my voice to those
of others in my study group who couldn't find a time to meet.

It was shortly after my achievement of becoming as overburdened as my colleagues that our study group collapsed. We

all agreed that we didn't have enough time to continue on. We were too busy, too successful to be able to sit down together, drink coffee on Sunday mornings, and talk and reflect.

It was about this time that I began thinking about writing about Brenda and the women in my groups. It took me quite a bit longer to connect my patients' experience to my own.

Many of us have come to avoid, perhaps even to fear, leisure. For some, having free time has become a sign of professional inadequacy. It means that we are unimportant, of lesser status. In order to compensate for that feeling of inadequacy, we forego drinking coffee and musing about the world with friends in order to prove to ourselves and others that we are worthy by working on Sundays. For some, having time away from work is time to feel lonely or to look inward and find dissatisfaction. For others, it signals an absence of meaning, a feeling of not knowing what to do.

Given our investment in work, many of us have little experience in cultivating leisure time outside of watching television or shopping. If we are constantly at work, preparing for work, recovering from work, we can say to ourselves that we will think about our lives when we have time, when life isn't so hectic. We put our dreams, our fantasies, our needs for intimacy and friendship, our desire to be cared for or attended to, on hold. We postpone having fun, hanging out, reflecting on life, into an indeterminate future. We become emotional ascetics and put up with remarkably deprived, driven, and insular lives. We allow ourselves to pretend that commodities will fill the gaps, provide meaning. However, with each acquisition, the gratification, the fix, is short lived. If we're honest with ourselves, we know that consuming isn't the answer.

When attempting to understand Americans' obsession with work, theorists show a fair amount of contempt for us as a people. We are "trapped in the cycle of work-and-spend," and need to realize that "the culprit isn't out *there*—not in the global corporations, greedy executives, insensitive elites, immigrants, or poor minorities. It's in *here,* in our own appetites, in what we want to buy, in the great deals we want to get." However, what I see from my vantage point as a psychotherapist, listening day after day to people's hidden longings, fears, resentments, and shame-drenched feelings and thoughts is this: No one comes to therapy to complain about problems with shopping, about acquiring material things. They come to talk about what they feel they cannot discuss outside of the sanctity of the consulting room, with its promise of confidentiality and lack of judgmentalism. They come to find acceptance or understanding for what they experience as unspeakable, weak, shameful, childish, pathetic, uncivilized, or wrong. And, more likely than not, that leads us into a discussion not about greed and unfulfilled appetites, but about needs for closeness, acceptance, meaning, recognition, and care. All of those things that we as a nation of autonomous, independent men and women are increasingly supposed to do without.

As long as we think of ourselves as a people who are shallow, fundamentally consumerist, and blindly self interested, we will continue to overlook the psychological needs for connection, meaning, and attention that drive us. As long as our leaders maintain that Americans want nothing more than tax cuts and the reduction of the role of big government in their lives, we will not be called upon to think of ourselves as anything more than unconnected consumers who conflate citizenship with consumerism. As long as we deny *interdependence*—our dependence on each other—as the bedrock of life, we slip further into our private, isolated despair and insecurity. The more we allow the indifferent and nonbinding relationships of the market to further seep into all aspects of our lives, the more our personal commitments to one another will resemble market transactions. We will have less to come home to and less to go out to, and we will cleave to our jobs with greater need.

At present we are a society filled with fear—of faceless terrorism, of religious fanatics, of nations and of people who despise us. We are also, however, a society that fears free time. We fear that without our employers requiring us to be at work by 8:00 A.M. there will be no one else who truly needs us. We fear that without rushing to meet deadlines, our lives will feel empty. We fear that without the mandates of our employers, we will have no purpose. And our fears may be justified.

Americans have grown tolerant of living with these fears and pretending that they don't exist. Surrounded by our incomparable standard of living, our jobs, our things, we have convinced ourselves that intimacy, friendship, neighborliness, citizenship, attention, care, and leisure don't matter all that much. We perpetuate this denial at our peril. Life in the twenty-first century is not turning out to be what any of us expected. Perhaps finding ways of connecting with, committing to, and caring about each other is the highest goal to which we can aspire, both as individuals and as a society. Certainly, living to work not only stymies this goal but prevents us from asking ourselves how life should be lived and to whom we matter.

Are You Married to Your Job?

If you answer yes to 7 or more of the following statements, you may be too emotionally invested in your job.

1. The company I work for is like a family.

2. I feel compelled to check my work e-mail and voice mail when I'm away from work.

3. I feel guilty when I can't go to work (e.g., when I'm ill; when I have to pick up my kids from school).

4. I'd never consider looking for another job.

5. I would feel lonely without my job.

6. One of the best things about my work is getting my boss's approval.

7. I give over 100% of my effort at work.

8. No one in my personal life counts on me like they do at work.

9. I almost never take the full number of vacation days available to me for the year.

10. I feel I work harder than most of my coworkers.

11. I'm lucky to have the job I have.

12. Weekends are difficult for me.

13. I care more about what other people at work think about me than what my friends or neighbors think.

14. I go to bed at night thinking about work.

15. The thought of leaving my job fills me with dread.

16. My closest friends are at work.

Notes

INTRODUCTION

PAGE

2 People demonstrated their status: Joanne Ciulla, *The Working Life: The Promise and Betrayal of Modern Work* (New York: Times Books, 2000), p. 190.

3 A recent *New York Times* survey: Andrew Cherlin, "I'm O.K., You're Selfish," *New York Times Magazine* (10/17/99), p. 46.

3 According to the United Nations: International Labor Organization website, Press Release of 8/31/01.

3 Now we work on average: Steven Greenhouse, "Report Shows Americans Have More 'Labor Days,'" *New York Times,* 9/1/01.

3 Between 1977 and 1997: James Lardner, "World-class Workaholics," *US News and World Report* (12/20/99), p. 42.

3 A study of American workers found: Cited in Arlie Hochschild, *The Time Bind: When Work Becomes Home and Home Becomes Work* (New York: Metropolitan Books, 1997), p. 28.

3 In another survey, which asked workers whether they preferred a shorter work week: Ibid, p. 33.

4 A 2001 study of full- and part-time: Quoted in *The Wirthlin Report,* Vol. 11, No. 2, March 2001, p. 3.

4 In a comparative international survey: Robert Reich, *The Future of Success* (New York: Alfred Knopf, 2001), pp. 129–30.

4 When working mothers are offered choices: Hochschild, *The Time Bind,* op cit., pp. 28, 34.

4 Since 1973, free time has fallen: Juliet Schor, *The Overworked American: The Unexpected Decline of Leisure* (New York: Basic Books, 1992), p. 22.

4 According to a survey by Expedia.com: Cited in "Americans Get Less—and Don't Use It All," *San Francisco Chronicle,* 7/1/01.

4 As a study by AT&T discovered: Cited in Jerry Useem, "Welcome to the New Company Town," *Fortune Magazine,* January 10, 2000, p. 67.

5 Benjamin Hunnicutt, an historian of work: Quoted in Useem, Ibid.

CHAPTER ONE:
Married to the Job

PAGE

32 "Failure is the great modern taboo: Richard Sennett, *The Corrosion of Character: The Personal Consequences of Work in the New Capitalism* (New York: W.W. Norton, 1998), p. 118.

CHAPTER TWO
Less To Come Home to/
Less To Go Out to

PAGE

36 "Work as a concept: Jonathan Keats, "It's The End of Work As We Know It," *San Francisco Magazine,* December 1998, p. 45.

36 Until quite recently, social theorist Max Horkheimer's: Max Horkheimer, "Authority and the Family," *Critical Theory: Selected Essays* (New York: The Seabury Press, 1972), p. 118.

37 "For the first two-thirds: Robert Putnam, *Bowling Alone: The Collapse and Revival of American Community* (New York: Simon & Schuster, 2000), p. 27.

37 As author Brian Robertson has noted: Brian Robertson, *There's No Place Like Work: How Business, Government, and Our Obsession with Work Have Driven Parents from Home* (Dallas, TX: Spence Publishing Company, 2000), p. 95.

41 "To be a man one had to be: Jessie Bernard, "The Good-Provider Role: Its Rise and Fall," *American Psychologist,* Vol. 36, No. 1 (January 1981), p. 4.

41 As Barbara Ehrenreich points out: Barbara Ehrenreich, *The Hearts of Men: American Dreams and the Flight from Commitment* (Garden City, NY: Anchor/Doubleday, 1983), p. 7.

42 In comparing attitudinal surveys: Bernard, op cit., p. 8.

42 Bernard concludes that: Ibid, p. 2.

42 "In the 1950s . . . there was a firm expectation: Ehrenreich, op cit., pp. 11–12.

43 Once the marital tie is broken: Barbara Dafoe Whitehead, *The Divorce Culture: Rethinking Our Commitments to Marriage and Family* (New York: Vintage Books, 1996), p. 155.

43 A national survey of one thousand children: Reported in Frank Furstenberg and Kathleen Mullen Harris, "The Disappearing American Father? Divorce and the Waning Significance of Biological Parenthood," unpublished manuscript, University of Pennsylvania, Department of Sociology.

44 Sociologists Frank Furstenberg and Andrew Cherlin: Frank Furstenberg and Andrew Cherlin, *Divided Families: What Happens to Children When Parents Part* (Cambridge, MA: Harvard University Press, 1991), p. 36.

44 In 1950, 12.6 percent of women: Reported in Hochschild, *The Time Bind,* op cit., p. 6.

44 By 1998, 73 percent did: Reported in the *San Francisco Chronicle,* 10/24/00, and Susan Greenberg, "Time to Plan Your Life," *Newsweek,* 1/29/01.

44 While the sociological literature makes clear: See Putnam, op cit., p. 197, and Elliott Currie, et al., "The Fading Dream: Economic Crisis and the New Inequality," in Karen Hansen and Ilene Philipson (eds.), *Women, Class, and the Feminist Imagination* (Philadelphia, PA: Temple University Press, 1990), pp. 322–23.

44 Due to oil price increases: Schor, op cit., pp. 79–80 *passim.*

46 "It is always the first task of a movement: Barbara Easton (Epstein), "Feminism and the Contemporary Family," *Socialist Review,* 8:3, May–June 1978, pp. 12–13, 28.

47 "The chances are . . . you'll stay: David Viscott, *Feel Free: How to Do Everything You Want Without Feeling Guilt* (New York: Dell Publishing, 1971), pp. 9–10.

48 Divorce rates doubled in ten years: Whitehead, op cit., pp. 3, 76–77.

48 The proportion of people who are currently married: Putnam, op cit., p. 277.

48 In 1957, 53 percent of Americans: Cited in Ehrenreich, op cit., p. 120.

48 In 1972, 45 percent of American: Reported in the *New York Times,* 5/15/01.

49 In 1960, 13 percent of all households: Reported in the *New York Times,* 3/9/00.

52 Today, fathers of children under 18: Based on a 1997 report of the International Labor Organization reported in Barbara Kantowitz and Pat Wingert, "The Parent Trap," *Newsweek,* 1/29/01.

52 Married couples averaged fourteen: Putnam, op cit., p. 191.

53 And one-fifth of all working parents: Hochschild, *The Time Bind,* op cit., pp. 36–37.

53 The White House Council of Economic Advisers: Reich, *The Future of Success,* op cit., p. 119.

53 "[T]he most alarming development: Schor, op cit., p. 12.

53 A recent report from the Census Bureau: Kristin Smith, "Who's Minding the Kids? Child Care Arrangements: Fall 1995," reported in *The National Report on Work & Family,* 13:22 (11/14/00), p. 206.

53 At the same time, the average American teenager: Putnam, op cit, p. 264.

54 "Virtually all forms of family togetherness: Ibid, p. 101.

54 Over the last twenty years, married couples: Putnam, op cit., p. 100.

54 By 1997, spending on take-out: Reich, *The Future of Success,* op cit., p. 171.

54 These facts lead Robert Putnam: Putnam, op cit., pp. 100–101.

54 The average single-family house increased: Reported in the *New York Times,* 3/9/00.

54 Witold Rybcznski, author of *Home:* Quoted in the *New York Times,* 3/9/00.

55 The average American watches television: Putnam, op cit., pp. 222–23.

57 In one of the first surveys of the effects of Internet use: Reported in the *New York Times,* 2/16/00.

59 "In the grip of a time bind: Hochschild, *The Time Bind,* op cit., 228.

60 In *The Working Life:* Ciulla, op cit., p. 186.

60 For example, in 1986: Ibid, p. 194.

60 In March 2000, the *New York Times:* Katie Hafner, "For the Well Connected, All the World's an Office," *New York Times,* 3/30/00.

62 Dinesh D'Souza notes that, due to these technologies: Dinesh D'Souza, "Is Ecommerce Worth Dying For?" *Business* 2.0, 2/6/01, p. 82.

63 Judith Kaufman, who helped open: Quoted in the *San Francisco Chronicle,* 11/22/00.

63 Playground Connections: Hochschild, *The Time Bind,* op cit., 231.

63 Joanne Ciulla observes that the "more: Ciulla, op cit., p. 186.

69 Based on his review of surveys from the last quarter: Putnam, op cit., p. 100.

69 In the 1990s, Americans entertained: Ibid, p. 98.

69 A survey of Americans' readiness: Cited in Ibid, p. 100.

69 In an article in the *Wall Street Journal: Wall Street Journal,* 3/3/00.

70 Between 1974 and 1998: Putnam, op cit., pp. 105–6.

70 According to Putnam, "in the ten short: Ibid, p. 60.

71 These changes prompt Robert Putnam: Ibid, pp. 101–2.

72 In his thoughtful essay "The Fall of Fun": James Atlas, "The Fall of Fun," *The New Yorker,* 11/18/96, pp. 71, 62, 68.

72 Sociologist Arlie Hochschild echoes: Hochschild, *The Time Bind,* op cit., p. 229.

74 With the decline of family, neighborhood: Richard Sennett, "The New Political Economy and Its Culture," *The Hedgehog Review,* 2:1, Spring 2000, p. 66.

CHAPTER THREE
The Glue That Holds the Self Together

PAGE

82 Psychoanalyst Heinz Kohut: Heinz Kohut, *How Does Analysis Cure?* (Chicago: The University of Chicago Press, 1984), p. 47.

82   Stephen Mitchell, another psychoanalytic: Stephen Mitchell, *Relational Concepts in Psychoanalysis* (Cambridge, MA: Harvard University Press, 1988), pp. 33, 34–35.

85   "Without this selfobject experience: Howard Bacal, "The Centrality of Selfobject Experience in Psychological Relatedness," *Psychoanalytic Dialogues,* 5:3, 1995, p. 406.

85   We can move freely: Mitchell, op cit., p. 149.

89   "To the extent that one is surrounded: Kenneth Gergen, "The Self: Death by Technology," *The Hedgehog Review,* Vol. 1, Fall 1999, pp. 31–32.

91   "The single most important variable: Tony Schwartz, "The Greatest Sources of Satisfaction in the Workplace are Internal and Emotional," *Fast Company,* November 2000, p. 400.

97   "based on a 'parental model': Jerald Wallulis, *The New Insecurity: The End of the Standard Job and Family* (Albany, NY: SUNY Press, 1998), p. 93.

98   in what author Daniel Pink calls: Daniel Pink, *Free Agent Nation: How America's New Independent Workers are Transforming the Way We Live* (New York: Warner Books), 2001.

98   "Increasingly in the new economy: Reich, *The Future of Success,* op cit., pp. 132, 154.

98   As management guru Tom Peters: Tom Peters, "The Brand Called You," *Fast Company,* August–September 1997, pp. 83, 94.

99   "Today," Robert Reich announces: Robert Reich, "*Your* Job Is Change," *Fast Company,* October 2000, pp. 143–47 *passim.*

99   In fact, Reich insists it is crucial: Ibid, p. 150.

99   "The game is changing: Ibid, p. 154.

101   "In the eighties and early nineties: Malcolm Gladwell, "Designs for Working," *The New Yorker,* 12/11/00, p. 62.

103   "According to a 1999 survey: Putnam, op cit., p. 92.

104   "When the personality is for sale: Reich, *The Future of Success,* op cit., p. 156.

107   "As a path to happiness: Sigmund Freud, *Civilization and Its Discontents* (London: Hogarth Press, 1930), p. 80.

107   As one of the very few clinicians writing about work: Steven Axelrod, *Work and the Evolving Self: Theoretical and Clinical Considerations* (Hillsdale, NJ: The Analytic Press, 1999), p. 35.

107   Author Vince Bielski adds: Vince Bielski, "Our Magnificent Obsession," *Family Therapy Networker,* March–April 1996, p. 25.

109   Richard Sennett writes "Today": Richard Sennett, "The New Political Economy and Its Culture," op cit., p. 65.

CHAPTER FOUR
On the Difference Between Eggs and Bacon
PAGE

112 As *Fortune* magazine declared: Useem, op cit., p. 63.

113 "A robust culture: Terrence Deal and Allan Kennedy, *The New Corporate Cultures: Revitalizing the Workplace After Downsizing, Mergers, and Reengineering* (Reading, MA: Perseus Books, 1999), p. 3.

113 "A century ago the most valuable: Robert Levering and Milton Moskowitz, "The 100 Best Companies," *Fortune,* 1/10/00, p. 83.

113 In their book *The New Corporate Cultures:* Deal and Kennedy, op cit., p. 21.

114 Starbucks CEO Howard Schultz: Cited in ibid, p. 22.

114 Herb Kelleher, CEO of Southwest: Ibid.

114 In order to facilitate this belief: Ibid, p. 8.

116 "The Old Way: *Business 2.0,* 2/6/01, p. 77.

122 As real family life declines: Keats, op cit., pp. 44–45.

123 During a recent attempt to unionize: Reported in the *New York Times,* 8/10/97, p. 10.

123 According to Steelcase's Dave Lathrop: Quoted in Dave Arnott, *Corporate Cults: The Insidious Lure of the All-Consuming Organization* (New York: Amacom, 2000), p. 66.

123 At the software company PeopleSoft: Quoted in Quentin Hardy, "A Software Star Sees Its 'Family' Culture Turn Dysfunctional," *Wall Street Journal,* 5/5/99.

123 And when queried about work–family balance: Quoted in Useem, op cit, p. 64.

124 According to sociologist Helen Mederer: Quoted in ibid, p. 63.

124 "Pick just about any aspect: Ibid, p. 64.

124 "Aetna, Eastman Kodak: Robertson, op cit., p. 115.

125 According to Pam Belluck: Pam Belluck, "A Little Bit of Burping is O.K., If It Keeps Parents on the Job," *New York Times,* 12/4/00.

125 Given that "many offices these days: Lisa Foderaro, "In More Office Cubicles, the Dog Has Its Day," *New York Times,* 7/6/99.

125 As one employee interviewed by sociologist Arlie Hochschild: Hochschild, *The Time Bind,* op cit., p. 21.

126 I assume this is the motivation: Reported in Arnott, op cit., p. 3.

127 Although Americans enjoy far fewer holidays: See Schor, op cit., Chapter 3.

129 USAA Insurance in San Antonio: Arnott, op cit., p. 72.

129 Cisco Systems: Reported in Martin Miller, "Blue Year's Eve," *Los Angeles Times,* 12/5/99.

130 "Two years ago: Gladwell, op cit., p. 66.

131 "thriving little civil societies: Useem, op cit., 64.

132 Michael Novak, in his book: Michael Novak, *Business as a Calling* (New York: Free Press, 1996), pp. 146, 150.

132 Jay Conger, in *Spirit at Work:* Ciulla, op cit., p. 221.

132 Many studies have shown that: Putnam, op cit., p. 90.

133 "Working all the time: Jordana Willner, "Why Go Home While the Office Beckons?" *San Francisco Chronicle,* 1/30/00.

133 Given the decreased opportunities for the satisfaction: See Hochschild, *The Time Bind,* op cit., p. 42; and Deal and Kennedy, op cit., p. 6.

134 "Winning Spirit Awards: Deal and Kennedy, op cit., p. 8.

138 "Something is happening: Alan Webber and Bill Taylor, "Fast Company Manifesto," *Fast Company,* Vol. 1, No. 1, 1995.

139 "In ancient times: Dinesh D'Souza, op cit., 82.

139 "By car, by plane: Po Bronson, *Nudist on the Late Shift* (New York: Random House, 1999), pp. 3–4.

140 Business magazines, such as the new economy's: *Fast Company,* October 2000.

140 "You can become the author: William Taylor, "You Say You Want a Revolution?" *Fast Company,* October 2000, p. 90.

141 "Our mission is to make intelligence: Quoted in Chuck Salter, "People and Technology," *Fast Company,* April 2000, p. 192.

142 "For many, joining a startup: David Saks, "Startups Revive Workers of the World," *San Francisco Chronicle,* 12/21/99.

143 "Inside the bleak: Ciulla, op cit., pp. 134–5.

145 "Giving teams more control: Charles Derber, *Corporate Nation* (New York: St. Martin's Griffin, 1998), pp. 237, 238.

146 According to Richard Sennett: Sennett, "The New Political Economy and Its Culture," op cit., p. 66.

CHAPTER FIVE
Why Women?

PAGE

149 Although actual women exist: Jean Baker Miller, *Toward a New Psychology of Women* (Boston: Beacon Press, 1976), p. 48.

150 girls develop "with a basis for 'empathy: Nancy Chodorow, *The Repro-*

duction of Mothering (Berkeley, CA: University of California Press, 1978), pp. 167, 169.

151 On virtually every empirical indicator: See Putnam, op cit., p. 95.

155 "For women, in particular: Hochschild, *The Time Bind,* op cit., p. 201.

156 "The reality is that marriage: Quoted in Tamala Edwards, "Flying Solo," *Time Magazine,* 8/28/00, pp. 48, 50.

156 "For women as a group: Ehrenreich, op cit., p. 175.

156 Today, one-third of all children: See Reich, *The Future of Success,* op cit., p. 167.

157 "The result of divorce: Ehrenreich, op cit., p. 121.

157 When women work full time: See Louis Uchitelle, "Women Forced to Delay Retirement," *New York Times,* 6/26/01.

157 This economic inequality ends up: Reich, *The Future of Success,* op cit., p. 168.

162 In their book *The Minimal Family:* Jan Dizard and Howard Gadlin, *The Minimal Family* (Amherst, MA: The University of Massachusetts Press, 1990), pp. 6–7.

162 "Most Americans are so accustomed: Ibid, pp. 7–8.

163 In *The Second Shift:* Arlie Hochschild, *The Second Shift* (New York: Avon Books, 1989), pp. 3–4.

165 Arlie Hochschild notes that, today: Ibid, p. 247.

165 And, it was women who preserved this haven: Ibid, p. 241.

168 A "commuter train is filled: Ibid, p. 244.

169 Teamwork, recognition ceremonies: See Hochschild, *The Time Bind,* op cit., p. 20.

175 "Gradually I came to realize: Betty Friedan, *The Feminine Mystique* (New York: Dell Publishing, 1974), pp. 15, 21.

176 Compelled to put all of their energies: Ibid, p. 11.

178 "The world is going through more fundamental: Tom Peters, "What Will We Do For Work?," *Time Magazine,* 5/22/00, pp. 69–70.

181 As Arlie Hochschild has pointed out: Hochschild, *The Second Shift,* op cit., p. 11.

Chapter Six: Living to Work or Working to Live

Page

183 "Talk has always been the single: Quoted in Vince Bielski, op cit., p. 35.

191 "If change occurs it happens: Sennett, *The Corrosion of Character,* op cit., p. 148.

191 "the provision of the possibility: Harry Guntrip, *Psychoanalytic Theory, Therapy and the Self* (New York: Basic Books, 1971), p. 182.

191 "one of the few sanctuaries left: Bielski, op cit., 35.

203 According to psychoanalyst Andrew Morrison: Andrew Morrison, "The Breadth and Boundaries of a Self-Psychological Immersion in Shame: A One-and-a-Half-Person Perspective," *Psychoanalytic Dialogues,* 4:1, 1994, p. 24.

204 Given that shame is a relatively: Helen Block Lewis, "Shame—the 'Sleeper' in Psychopathology," in Helen Lewis (ed.), *The Role of Shame in Symptom Formation* (Hillsdale, NJ: Lawrence Earlbaum Associates, 1987), p. 18.

204 "Like fog, shame distorts: Morrison, op cit., pp. 19–20.

206 "What emerges most strongly: Bielski, op cit., p. 32.

207 "both enables and requires persons: Malcolm Pines, "The Self as a Group: The Group as a Self," Irene Harwood and Malcolm Pines (eds.), *Self Experiences in Group* (London: Jessica Kingsley Publishers, 1998), pp. 26–27.

216 "In times like these, the trained therapeutic: Bielski, op cit., p. 30.

Chapter Seven: Escape from Freedom

Page

222 "The structure of modern society: Erich Fromm, *Escape from Freedom* (New York: Henry Holt and Company, 1969), p. 104.

224 When Fromm wrote during the Second: Ibid, p. 4.

224 "the powerlessness and insecurity: Ibid, pp. 255–56.

226 0=best: Po Bronson, personal communication.

227 "Who needs me?: Sennett, *The Corrosion of Character,* op cit., p. 146.

228 When Rush Limbaugh suggested: Rush Limbaugh, *The Way Things Ought to Be* (New York: Pocket Books, 1992), p. 146.

229 "The social bond arises most elementally: Sennett, *The Corrosion of Character,* op cit., pp. 139, 141.

229 "The long-held promise: Bielski, op cit., 29.

234 We are "trapped in the cycle: Schor, op cit., p. 126.

234 "the culprit isn't out *there:* Reich, *The Future of Success,* op cit., p. 240.

Acknowledgments

I wish to thank my patients—the women and men who have come to my office to discuss their problems at work—in the writing of this book. I particularly wish to thank the early members of my "Women and Work" groups for their patience with me, as I gradually came to understand and to empathize. Starting in 1993, many of them began to urge me to write about the phenomenon they were experiencing, to get the message out. Despite the amount of time it has taken me to respond to their call, I hope they find what I have written to be a satisfactory rendering. I have learned so much from them. I particularly wish to thank Janel, Gennette, Dee, Anita, Rosanna, Katherine, Sandra, Iris, Veronica, Donna, Yolanda, Vikki, Pamela, Marilyn, Wendy, and Jennifer. I also wish to thank Andrea, Scott, Lori, and Bernadette.

My writers' group has been invaluable to me. I would like to acknowledge Barbara Epstein, Gayle Greene, Sheryy Keith, and Kay Trimberger for their support, critique and provocation. I'd particularly like to thank Gayle and Kay for their help and companionship at every step of this process.

My intellectual home throughout the writing of this book has been the Center for Working Families at UC Berkeley. I'd like to thank Arlie Hochschild and Barrie Thorne for creating such a collegial environment. It is Arlie's work that provided me with a sociological framework for understanding what I was listening to daily in my clinical practice. Her ideas are reflected throughout this book, and I owe her a substantial intellectual debt.

For their various contributions, I wish to thank Michael Black, Zelda Bronstein, Bob Dunn, Ron Elson, Jeffrey Escoffier, Karen Hansen, Jane Jordan, Pam Kruger, Shelley Podolny, Geoff Smith, Jerry Useem, Randy Wyatt, and Archie. I also wish to thank my editor, Rachel Klayman, and my agent, Peter Ginsberg.

Finally, I wish to thank Jim Stockinger, who has been my intellectual and emotional terra firma throughout the writing of this book. The passion and joy he brings to my life insures that I will never marry any job.

Index

About the Author

Ilene Philipson holds doctorates in both sociology and clinical psychology, and has taught at UC Berkeley, UC Santa Cruz, and New York University. Currently in private practice, she is the author of three previous books including *Ethel Rosenberg: Beyond the Myths* and *On the Shoulders of Women: The Feminization of Psychotherapy,* and is a research affiliate at the Center for Working Families at UC Berkeley. She lives in Berkeley, California.